Louisiana Life Series, No. 2

Cajun Music

Its Origins and Development

by Barry Jean Ancelet

D1523370

Published by The Center for Louisiana Studies
University of Southwestern Louisiana
Lafayette, Louisiana

for Caroline

Library of Congress Catalog Number: 89-60537
ISBN Number: 0-940984-48-2

Copyright 1989
University of Southwestern Louisiana

The Center for Louisiana Studies
P.O. Box 40831
University of Southwestern Louisiana
Lafayette, LA   70504

Contents

Acknowledgements

The University of Southwestern Louisiana has provided ongoing support for this research and related projects since I first joined the faculty in 1977. The University's Center for Acadian and Creole Folklore received a grant from the Rockefeller Foundation (1977-78) which funded new field research, as well as a project to locate and acquire past research on Louisiana French folklore and folklife, much of which was on Cajun and zydeco music. A grant from the National Endowment for the Humanities (1979-82) made it possible to continue this initial effort. The Council for the Development of French in Louisiana funded preliminary fieldwork, especially through the Tribute to Cajun Music festival (1974-80). The Lafayette Jaycees, who later assumed sponsorship of the festival, now called Festival de Musique Acadienne, have contributed some of the proceeds each year (1980-present) to fund fieldwork and other projects including the acquisition of past collections, especially the 1934-37 Lomax collection from the Library of Congress. The Louisiana Division of the Arts/Louisiana State Arts Council funded further research on the Lomax collection which resulted in a double album released by Swallow Records (LP 8003-2).

Parts of this book are based on an earlier draft which was included in "The Cajuns: Their History and Culture," a five-volume research report prepared for Hamilton and Associates (1986-87) as part of the plans to develop three Acadian culture centers within the Jean Lafitte National Historical Park and Preserve, and funded by the National Park Service/United States Department of the Interior.

Mathé Allain, Carl Brasseaux and Glenn Conrad have contributed personally and professionally to my understanding of Cajun music by guiding me in an exploration of its historical context. Elemore Morgan, Jr., Carl Lindahl, Philip Gould, James Edmunds, Marc and Ann Savoy, Dewey Balfa, David Barry, Nicholas Spitzer, Alan Lomax, Ray Brassieur, Joe Wilson and Ralph Rinzler have helped me to keep current developments in perspective over the years with valuable questions and thought provoking observations.

Finally, anyone who writes about Cajun music owes a debt of gratitude to the fiercely independent musicians who thankfully have never listened to folklorists, anthropologists and ethnomusicologists and continue to perform in a way that is rooted in the cultural bedrock, yet soars with creative originality.

Cajun Music:

Its Origins and Development

Like most other features of Louisiana French culture, Cajun music is the product of creolization. Cajun music is a blend of German, Spanish, Scottish, Irish, Anglo-American, Afro-Caribbean and American Indian influences with a base of western French and French Acadian folk tradition. *Zydeco/zarico,** the most contemporary expression of black Creole music, and its precursors, *la-la* and *juré,* developed from the same set of influences with a heavier dose of Afro-Caribbean rhythms and styles. Both traditions were built by musicians with little or no formal training who improvised the music of their generation out of the ones that came before them. Cajun music differs substantially from the traditional music of its sister French-American cultures in Quebec, New Brunswick, Nova Scotia, New England and even Missouri because none of these other places had the unique blend of ingredients found in South Louisiana. Further, Cajun music, like *zydeco/zarico,* was born in exile, of ancient traditions which found themselves displaced, in a New World where old ways did not stand in the way of new combinations.

In the earliest period of French influence, beginning in 1682 when La Salle claimed Louisiana for France, and the first efforts at colonization in 1699, there was obviously little music. Louisiana was explored and colonized primarily by men who had already been changed by the frontier and were no longer French but French-Canadians. The most important aspect of this new North American experience was personal freedom. Away from the constraints of the complex European system, the early settlers began to create a new identity for themselves to coincide with life in the New World. This new life depended only on their abilities and ambitions. They were free to take as big a bite as they thought they could chew. This personal freedom was reflected in the folklore and traditions of the settlers. Their oral tradition began to include a large repertoire of tall tales, in addition to their western European stock of animal tales and fairy tales. Their songs began to include bawdy and humorous songs as well as the

*The spelling of *zydeco* was coined in 1960 by Mack McCormick, an ethnomusicologist in Houston who was attempting to render phonetically the term that black Creole musicians were using to identify their music. *Zarico* is a more recent, French phonetic rendering by André Gladu, a French Canadian.

1

traditional ballads brought from France. Some of the oldest songs reflected
the settlers' European origins. They sang unaccompanied ballads which told
of wives and wars and faraway lands. Songs like "Malbrough s'en va-t-
guerre," "La Guerre de sept ans," "Trois jolis tambours," and "La Belle et le
capitaine," reflect the history and tradition of the Old World:

Le plus jeune des trois
L'a pris par sa main blanche.

"Montez, montez, la belle,
Dessus mon cheval gris.
Au logis chez mon père,
Je vous emmènerai."

Quand la belle-z-entend,
La belle est tombée morte.

"Sonnez, sonnez les cloches.
Tambours, violons, marchez.
Ma mignonette est morte.
J'en ai le cœur dolent.

"Et où l'enterreront-ils?"
"Dedans le jardin de son père
Sous les trois feuilles de lys.
Nous prions Dieu, cher frère,
Qu'elle aille en paradis."

Au bout de trois jours,
La belle frappe à la porte.

"Ouvrez, ouvrez la porte,
Cher papa et bien aimé.
J'ai fait la morte trois jours
Pour sauver mon honneur."

(Traditional, as sung by Julien Hoffpauir, New Iberia, 1934; Lomax
collection/Archive of Folk Song [AFS] 32a1; *Louisiana Cajun and Creole
Music, 1934: The Lomax Recordings,* Swallow 8003-2.)

Some songs coincided with contemporary preoccupations in the New World. "Tout un beau soir en me promenant" describes a meeting between a woodsman and a shepherdess on the edge of an enchanted woods. She tells him that if he will spare the trees, she will keep his glass filled with wine.

Tout un beau soir en me promenant
O tout du long du petit bois charmant,

'Garde, je vois là-bas, je vois venir une bergère.
Ça me fait rappeler la seule que mon cœur aime.

"Belle bergère, jolie bergère,
C'est quoi vous faîtes dedans ces bois?"

"J'ai mes moutons dedans ces plaines,
Là où le loup me fait souvent ouvrage."

Les beaux bûcheurs, ils sont partis au bois,
C'est pour couper la fleur du bois.

"Ne coupez pas ni la souche ni la retraite,
Vous goûterez du vin dans mes bouteilles."

"En buvons une, en buvons deux,
En buvons trois, o s'il le faut."

(Traditional, as sung by Elita Hoffpauir, New Iberia, 1934; Lomax/AFS 37a1; Swallow 8003-2.)

Another popular French song tradition transplanted to Acadia and Louisiana was the drinking song, called in the New World, *la chanson de bamboche.* This type of song was especially popular at social gatherings like Christmas and New Year celebrations, wedding receptions, and house dances, and some, like "Trinquons," were often repeated to mark the pouring of each new glass.

Trinquons, trinquons, mes chers camarades,
Mais oublions jamais la raison.
Soutenez mon verre et me voilà par terre.

Chantez de boire du matin au soir.
Que le tonnerre grogne et que la muraille recule.
Me voilà par terre du matin au soir.

(Traditional, as sung by Fenelus and Cleveland Sonnier, Erath, 1934;
Lomax/AFS 26a3; Swallow 8003-2.)

Some of these songs have survived until today. The universally known
"Chevaliers de la table ronde" is echoed in "Fais trois de la table ronde,"
which retains essential elements of the pre-Arthurian fisher king legend
which describes the efforts to revive the ailing king and his failing land by
questing. Meanwhile, the king is kept alive with a trickle of alcohol:

O fais trois tours de la table ronde,
Fais trois tours de la table ronde.
Allons en chercher, chercher, chercher, chercher.

O c'est quoi, se divertir, c'est comme des camarades,
C'est quoi, se divertir, c'est comme des camarades.
Allons en chercher, chercher, chercher, chercher.

Un de nos plus grands de nos ivrognes était au lit malade.
Mettez lui couché en bas d'une table de vin.
Allons en chercher, chercher, chercher, chercher.

Tous les temps en temps quittez une goutte dégouter,
Tous les temps en temps quittez une goutte dégouter.
Allons en chercher, chercher, chercher, chercher.

De leur quitter une goutte dégouter, c'est pour les satisfaire.
De leur quitter une goutte dégoutter, c'est pour les satisfaire.
Allons en chercher, chercher, chercher, chercher.

(As sung by Canray Fontenot, Welsh, 1977; Ancelet Collection, Folklore
Archives/University of Southwestern Louisiana [FA/USL].)

This theme is even found in contemporary dance music, as heard in the
Balfa Brothers "Parlez-nous à boire, non pas du mariage . . ." (*The Balfa*

Brothers Play Traditional Cajun Music, Swallow 6011) and *"La Danse de limonade"* (Nathan Abshire, *Pinegrove Blues,* Swallow 6014).

Founded in 1604, Port Royal was one of the first European settlements north of Mexico. Most of the settlers who eventually became the Acadians came from a twenty-five mile radius around Loudun in the province of Poitou in 1632. Other settlers came from Brittany, Normandy, and parts of southwestern France. Though they were primarily farmers at first, some already knew the ways of the sea and others soon came to learn them as fishermen on the Acadian peninsula. This maritime heritage is reflected in "Sept ans sur mer," a sailor's shanty about a shipwrecked family which is known all along the coast of Europe from the North Sea to the Mediterranean:

On a passé six ans sur mer
Sans pouvoir border la terre.

Au bout de la septième année,
On a manqué de provisions.

On a mangé souris et rats
Jusque le tourbe du navire.

On a tiré la courte paille
Pour voir lequel qui serait mangé.

O voilà petit Jean qu'il tombe au sort.
Ça serait petit Jean qui serait mangé.

O petit Jean, ça lui fait du mal.
Il crie, 'Courage, mes camarades.

'Je vois la terre sur toutes côtés,
Trois pigeons blancs qui sont à voltiger.

'Je vois aussi trois filles du prince
Qui se promenaient au long du rivage.

'O si jamais je mets les pieds sur terre,
La plus jolie, je l'épouserai.'

(Traditional, as sung by Elita Hoffpauir, New Iberia, 1934; Lomax/AFS
31a1; Swallow 8003-2)

Other traditions affected the Acadian repertoire as well. Some songs
apparently reflect the Celtic origins of some Acadian settlers. "Madame
Gallien," for example, portrays a mother who inadvertently makes a pact
with a faerie by wishing aloud while walking down a country lane:

Madame Gallien était promenant
Dans son jardin, son coeur bien chagrin.

Tout le long d'une allée,
Elle faisait que pleurer,

Toujours en espérant
Pierrot Grouillet pour se marier.
Pierrot Grouillet, il est arrivé.
Il dit, 'Josette, faut se marier.'

Tout chacun s'en va chez soi
Pour laisser savoir à tout,
Danse, sur le moment,
Monsieur le curé publiera les bans.

O son parrain, il la consentant,
Il dit, 'Moi, j'irai les mener.'

Deux vieux boeufs, deux vieux chevaux
Attelés sur un vieux chariot
Pour aller marier
Pierrot Grouillet et Mademoiselle Josette.

Dans le chemin, ils ont fait rencontre
D'un petit bonhomme,
Un pied chaussé et l'autre nu.

Son violon dans son bras,
Son archet dans sa main,
Il disait qu'il voulait jouer
Jusqu'à qu'il n'ait plus de souliers.

(Traditional, as sung by Lanese Vincent and Sidney Richard, Kaplan, 1934; Lomax/AFS 28b1; Swallow 8003-2.)

When the Acadians were exiled in 1755, they took with them few possessions, but did carry away a rich cultural heritage which included their persistent sense of identity based on a blend of French, Celtic, Scots-Irish, and Native American influences. This mixture came to be manifested in a rich oral tradition and a repertoire of songs and dances. Music for dancing was preserved in hummed *reels à bouche*. Sometimes, changes in tunes and lyrics reflected the New World and especially the new Louisiana context. In the French version of "Cadet Roussel," one finds features of traditional French architecture described in classic French grammar:

Cadet Roussel a trois maisons (bis)
Qui n'ont ni poutre ni chevrons. (bis)
C'est pour loger les hirondelles.
Que direz-vous de Cadet Roussel?

Ah, ah, ah oui vraiment,
Cadet Roussel est bon enfant.

In an early Louisiana version collected by Irene Whitfield Holmes during the 1930s, there are changes which reflect the *poteaux-en-terre* building technique used in New France and Acadia as well as more informal grammar:

Cadet Roussel a une maison, qui n'a ni poteaux, ni chevrons,
C'est pour loger les hirondelles, qui croyez-vous de cadet Roussel?

Ha, ha, ha, oui, vraiment. Cadet Roussel, c'est un bon garçon.

(Traditional, as transcribed in Irene Whitfield Holmes, *Louisiana French Folk Songs* [Baton Rouge: Louisiana State University Press, 1939].)

In a later version collected in Mamou during the early 1960s by Harry Oster, there are further modifications:

> Cadet Roussel, c'est un bon jeune homme,
> Cadet Roussel, c'est un vaillant bougre.
>
> Cadet Roussel, il la des chiens que le roi n'a pas de si bons,
> Un aux lapins et l'autre si bête que quand il l'appelle, il se sauve.
> Ah oui, vraiment.
>
> Cadet Rousel, il a une habille que le roi n'a pas de si belle.
> Elle est doublée de papier gris, elle est cousue de la ficelle.
> Ah oui, vraiment.
>
> Cadet Rouselle, il a des chevaux que le roi n'a pas des si bons.
> Ils sont si gras que les os percent la selle.
> Ah oui, vraiment.
>
> Cadet Rouselle, il a-t-un clos que le roi n'a pas des si grands.
> Il est si grand, il monte une face, il crache sur l'autre.
> Ah oui, vraiment.
>
> Cadet Rouselle, c'est un bon jeune homme.
> Cadet Rouselle, c'est un vaillant bougre.

(Traditional, as sung by Isom Fontenot, Mamou; Oster Collection, FA/USL; and on *Folksongs of the Louisiana Acadians,* Arhoolie 5009.)

There is no verse concerning his house in the entire text of this version, perhaps indicating that *poteaux-en-terre* proved to be a disastrous building practice in humid, termite-infested South Louisiana. There is also a definite creolization of vocabulary and grammar in this version.

Similarly, there is a noticeable change of vocabulary and style in the following versions of "Le Mariage des animaux." Versions collected in Quebec reflect the preservation of animals which were familiar to the settlers of New France:

> C'est un corbeau puis une corneille
> Qui voulaient bien se marier.

Mais ils voulaient bien faire des noces
Mais ils n'avaient pas de quoi manger.

Li lon la . . . il y en aura.

Mais ils voulaient bien faire des noces
Mais ils n'avaient pas de quoi manger.
Aperçoit venir un gros renard,
Trois quarts de lard dessus son corps.

Li lon la . . . il y en aura.

Mais pour du lard, nous en avons,
Mais c'est du pain que nous manquons.
Aperçoit venir un gros lapin,
Il tient un pain dessus ses reins.

Li lon la . . . il y en aura.

A version collected in Louisiana preserves the basic sequential structure of this song. Some of the characters are replaced with animals more familiar to the South Louisiana context. Others like the *corbigeau* reflect the Acadians' passage in Canada:

C'est la caille et la perdrix
Qui se marient, o oui lundi.
Du monde, nous avons assez.
C'est du vin qui nous manquera.

Leurreleurreleur, bel oiseau, à rien de plus beau.

Passe ici une souris, dessus son dos porte un barril.
Passe ici une souris, dessus son dos porte un barril.
Du monde et du vin, nous avons assez.
C'est de la viande qui nous manquera.

Leurreleurreleur, bel oiseau, à rien de plus beau.

Passe ici un corbigeau, dessus son dos porte un gigot.
Passe ici un corbigeau, dessus son dos porte un gigot.
Du monde et du vin et de la viande, nous avons assez.
C'est du pain qui nous manquera.

Leurreleurreleur, bel oiseau, à rien de plus beau.

Passe ici un pigeon, dedans son bec porte un pain long.
Passe ici un pigeon, dedans son bec porte un pain long.
Du monde et du vin et de la viande et du pain, nous avons assez.
C'est la musique qui nous manquera.

Leurreleurreleur, bel oiseau, à rien de plus beau.

Passe ici un gros rat, dessus son bras porte un violon.
Passe ici un gros rat, dessus son bras porte un violon.
Le gros chat qui est au grenier,
'Miaou, miaou, miaou. Miaou, miaou, miaou.
C'est pas mon violon que je regretterai,
Mais c'est mes os qui vont craler.'

Leurreleurreleur, bel oiseau, à rien de plus beau.

(Traditional, as sung by Sabry Guidry, Abbeville, 1976; Ancelet Collection, FA/USL.)

In some cases, only the kernel of the story survives. "Grand Dieu, que je suis à mon aise," a well-known French folksong, loses most of its direct references to European wars in the New World version. This excerpt from the typical French version includes specific European references:

Grand Dieu, que je suis à mon aise
Quand j'ai ma mie auprès de moi, auprès de moi.

De temps en temps, je la regarde
Et je lui dis, 'Embrasse-moi.'

'Comment veux-tu que je t'embrasse,
Quand on me dit du mal de toi, du mal de toi?

On me dit que tu pars pour la guerre
Chez les Flamands, défendre le roi.'

The following Louisiana version, sung in 1976 by Odile Falcon, of
Lafayette, is remarkably complete, though it generalizes the references to the
war:

Oh, Grand Dieu, comme je suis-t-à mon aise
Quand je la vois, elle assise auprès de moi.

'Temps en temps je vous regarde, ma douce aimée,
Oh, ma douce aimée, embrasse donc moi.'

'Oh, cher amant, comment tu veux moi, je t'embrasse
Quand on me défend de t'aimer tous les jours.

Un petit mot qui me monte à l'oreille,
C'était de me faire faire un petit portrait,

Un petit portrait de ta ressemblance
Et cent fois par jour, je l'embrasserai.'

'Q'est-ce que tes amis diraient de toi,
Te voir embrasser ce petit portrait?'

'Je leur dirai que c'est le portrait,
Que c'est le portrait de ma bien aimée

Que j'avais quittée d'un si grand regret
Pour partir servir sur l'armée régulière.

Oh maman, elle vena me souffler un petit mot à l'oreille
En me disant que j'étais parti,

J'étais parti pour servir le grand roi,

Servir le grand roi sur l'armée régulière.

(Traditional, as sung by Odile Falcon, Lafayette, 1976; Ancelet Collection, FA/USL)

Singers sometimes approximated unfamiliar sounds when they did not understand geographic references from the old country. "Le Pont de Nantes," a well-known French folksong about a bridge in one of the principal cities in Brittany, survived the Atlantic crossing under several titles, including "Au Pont des vues," "Au Pont du Nord," "Le Pont du Nane." One Louisiana singer, Inez Catalon, of Kaplan, omitted the first line reference to the bridge and began her version with the second line, "Bonjour, Hélène..."

Older French songs were often adapted to new styles or recent events. "La Veuve de sept ans," originally a *complainte* about two lovers separated during the Crusades, became in Acadia a song about the Seven Years' War:

J'avais une maîtgresse, un jour y avait longtemps.
J'ai reçu une lettre, 'En guerre il faut aller.'

Ma pauvre petite maîtresse ne fait que brailler
Tout la nuit et toute la journée.

'En guerre j'm'en vas, ma belle, j'reviens dans une semaine
Attendrir nos amours.'

Ça bien duré sept ans, pendant ma vingtième année
J'suis rentré en Acadie.

J'ai été voir ma belle qui pouvait pas me regarder.
Oh, la grande misère.

J'ai été voir ma mère qui braillait,
Mon père est mort, mes frères sont morts, ma terre ruinée
Ma belle mariée à cause de la maudite guerre.

Ecoutez-moi bien, jeunes gens,
Partez jamais à la guerre.

J'ai perdu mon père, perdu ma famille,
Ma terre est toute ruinée
A cause de la maudite guerre...

(Traditional, as sung by Pierre Robichaux, Moncton, New Brunswick; *1755*, Presqu'île Records)

A similar song in Louisiana has the maiden placed in a convent where she dies of a broken heart before her lover returns from his military campaign:

Une jeune fille de quatorze ans,
O oui, Grand Dieu, que la belle brune,
Un soir elle dit à son papa,
'Papa, je veux me marier.'
'Fillette, jeunesse, mais taisez-vous.
Vous n'avez pas encore quinze ans.
Vous n'avez pas encore quinze ans.
Pour plaire à-t-un amant.'
Quand la belle a entendu ce discours,
Elle a monté dans sa chaumière.
Ses beaux yeux noirs,
Elle les a essuyés.
Elle avait plus qu'un seul petit frère
Qui la reconsole nuit comme le jour.
'Ma chère soeur, reconsole-toi.
Papa te mettra au couvent,
Droit au couvent des orphelines
Là où ce qu'on prie le Dieu souvent.'
'Mais c'est celui que mon cœur aime.
Il est esclave dedans la guerre.'
J'ai été en guerre quatre ans de temps.
Je me suis battu de nuit et jour.
Quand je suis revenu de ma révolte,
Droite chez la belle, je m'en ai été.
En demandant, 'Et où la belle?
Et où la belle que j'aimais tant?
Ses beaux yeux noirs, je voudrais les voir,
Je voudrais les voir encore une fois.'
On m'a répond, 'Ta belle à toi,

Elle est plus là pour toi la voir.
Elle est morte et enterrée
Depuis trois jours, c'est pas longtemps.'
Bonsoir, la belle, pour la dernière fois.
T'es dans ta tombe, je t'aime encore.
Mes yeux pleureront de nuit et jour,
C'est pour la belle brune que j'aimais tant.
Je me ferai faire un grand crèpe noir
Pendant six mois je le porterai.

(Traditional, as sung by Julien Hoffpauir, New Iberia, 1934; Lomax/AFS 32b2; Swallow 8003-2.)

Still another Louisiana version presents the dilemma of the woman whose fiancé is called away to war on their wedding day. He comforts her saying that he will be back in six weeks, two months at the most, a line echoed by the Confederates as they left for the Civil War. Believing herself a widow after seven years, she remarries only to have her first husband return shortly after the wedding. She is then forced to choose between the two:

Dessus le premier jour des noces, il y a été venu un comandement,
Il y a été venu un comandement, o un commandement de guerre.
'C'est à la guerre il faut aller. C'est à la guerre il faut partir.'
O, quand la belle a entendu ça, elle se mit à se désoler.
'Ne pleurez pas autant la belle, ne versez pas autant de larmes.
O, ma campagne serait pas longue, six semaines à deux mois le plus.'
O, ma campagne, elle a bien été belle, elle a été belle et belle et longue.
O, ma campagne, elle a bien duré, o, regarde, elle a duré sept ans.
Au bout de la septième année, o, quand j'ai pu me retirer,
C'était revenir chez moi, c'était trouver la mariée.
C'était trouver ma bien aimée qui sortait d'être épousée.
Elle s'est tournée à sa mère, 'O, vierge, vierge, douce vierge,
Quoi ce qu'en deviendra de moi?
Regarde donc sept ans je me croyais veuve, et me voilà avec deux maris.'
'Courage, courage, courage, ma fille,
Que le premier choix de l'homme lui appartienne à lui ses droits.'

(Traditional, as sung by Agnes Bourque, New Iberia, 1974; Stanford Collection; *J'étais au bal*, Swallow 6020.)

Creolization has not only affected the texts of songs transplanted by the Acadian exiles and the French immigrants. One result of the blues influence in Louisiana French tradition occurs in the transformation of gay, lilting European melodies to soulful, plaintive tunes. "Mon petit mari," for example, which in the French version typically combines rather gruesome lyrics concerning the devouring of the diminutive husband by the housecat with a joyous tune, keeps basically the same storyline in the Acadian version, but the melody is altered to a more suitable, plaintive style. Even a *danse ronde* like "Ah mon beau château" in Louisiana sounds much more plaintive than its older European counterpart because of the addition of a blues seventh in the second line. The tunes of other well-known French *danses rondes,* or play party songs, like "Papillon, vole," "J'ai été-z au bal hier au soir" (not the contemporary dance tune of the same title), and "La Fête printanière" have been adapted to the singing style of the region which esteems an edge and a more bluesy sound than is found in France.

Early Louisiana French instrumental tradition was based on familiar instruments like the fiddle or violin. Yet it is doubtful that the earliest settlers or the Acadian exiles owned instruments. Earliest mention of instruments in Louisiana colonial records is in the succession of a fiddler and clarinetist in 1782. Western French instrumental tradition had included brass and reed instruments such as the *biniou* or *cabrette* (instruments of the bagpipe family found in Celtic and southwestern French traditions) and trumpets (widely used in Poitou). These instruments fell into disuse in the New World. Tunes were transferred to stringed instruments, yet retained a distinctive drone. The French *vielle à roue,* with its characteristic *bourdon* drone, was too complicated and delicate to survive frontier conditions, but early fiddlers playing in open tuning achieved a similar effect. By the time of the exile, English and Scots-Irish reels, jigs, hornpipes and *contredanses* had already enriched the Acadians' repertoire of dance music.

When instruments were unavailable or at special times, such as Lent, when instrumental music was forbidden, the Acadians managed to dance anyway, producing music with their voices, clapping their hands, and stamping their feet for percussion. If the repertoire of round dances became stale, they simply used their voices as instruments to produce dance tunes called *des reels à bouche.* Descriptions of the Acadians at the time of the dispersion invariably mention their insatiable love of dancing. In a letter to his intendant dated March 12, 1764, Saltoris described a communal wedding and baptism blessing ceremony among the Acadian exiles in Saint-

Domingue: "They did not eat until every one had given his toast. They danced, the old and the young alike, all dancing to a fast step." (Colonial Records Collection, Center for Louisiana Studies, University of Southwestern Louisiana) Later, in the early nineteenth century, this still held true. C. C. Robin's travel account from 1803-1805 maintains that the Acadians

> love to dance most of all; more than any other people in the colony. At one time during the year, they give balls for travelers and will go ten or fifteen leagues to attend one. Everyone dances, even grandmère and grandpère, no matter what the difficulties they must bear. There may be only a couple of fiddles to play for the crowd, there may be only four candles for light, placed on wooden arms attached to the wall; nothing but long wooden benches to sit on and only exceptionally a few bottles of tafia diluted with water for refreshment; no matter, everyone dances.

Acadian exiles began arriving in Louisiana in 1765, with the deliberate intention of recreating their society on French territory. The first to arrive, however, were surprised to find themselves under Spanish rule, Louisiana having been ceded to Spain in 1762. Yet Spanish language and culture prevailed only at the highest administrative level; everyday life in the colony continued to be essentially in French. The majority of the Acadians who came to Louisiana arrived between 1765 and 1785. The last groups came primarily by way of the Middle Atlantic colonies and France. An attempt to repatriate some of the exiles in France failed because, among other reasons, the Acadians were no longer interested in living in what amounted to a feudal system under the French monarchy. Many of these offered themselves to the king of Spain as settlers for his newly acquired colony in Louisiana. There they joined other Acadians in establishing what they called *la Nouvelle Acadie.*

The Acadians settled along the banks of the Mississippi River, Bayou Lafourche, and in the lands west of the Atchafalaya Basin near the Poste des Attakapas and the Poste des Opelousas. In all three areas they lived in relative (though not total) isolation and addressed themselves to the huge task of reestablishing their fractured society. Though songs about the exile experience do not seem to have survived, the upheaval would have an affect on their music. The sufferings they had endured endowed their songs with a preoccupation with death, loneliness and lost love and their instrumental music with a mournful quality.

In Louisiana, the Acadians continued to sing the old songs and they created new ones. Their self-imposed isolation in the bayous and southern prairies did not preclude selective contact with other cultures, when they needed or wanted to learn something from their neighbors. They learned agricultural techniques, for example, from the local Native American tribes and from the Alsatian/German community along the German Coast, fishing techniques from the Anglo-Americans, cooking techniques from the black slaves. Even the Spaniards, generally believed to have influenced only New Orleans architecture and the colonial political scene, contributed to the civilization of the frontier-minded Acadians at contact points like New Iberia and especially through the churches. The steady trickle of French immigrants in the nineteenth century brought some changes in language and customs.

The Acadians' contact with these various cultures also contributed to the development of new musical styles and repertoire. From the Indians, they apparently learned a terraced singing style and new dance rhythms; from the blacks, they learned the blues, percussion techniques, a love of syncopation and improvisational singing; from the Spanish, they may have learned a few tunes, including the melody to "J'ai passé devant ta porte" (used in a concerto for classical guitar by the eighteenth-century composer Frederico Sors). Refugees and their slaves who arrived from Saint-Domingue at the turn of the nineteenth century reinforced the African influence with a syncopated West Indian beat. The Jewish German immigrants began importing diatonic accordions (invented in Vienna in 1828) when Acadians and blacks became interested in the instruments toward the end of the nineteenth century. They blended these elements to create a new music just as they were synthesizing the same cultures to create Cajun society.

From the Anglo-American immigrants who arrived in increasing numbers throughout the late eighteenth and nineteenth centuries, they were to learn much including new fiddle tunes like Virginia reels, square dances and hoedowns, along with a few new ballads some of which they translated into French. A remarkable example of this is "J'ai marié un ouvrier," a Louisiana French version of the English ballad, "James Harris" or "The Demon Lover," sometimes known as "The Carpenter's Wife" (Child 243). In Louisiana, an *ouvrier* is not a general laborer, as in France, but specifically a carpenter. In this version a well-bred young wife, bored with her carpenter husband, is swept away by a sailor. When he brings her to the

port city, she learns that she is to sail with him. She then realizes that she
will never return to the family she has abandoned. The yellow silk dress he
offers her in consolation is mentioned in Scottish versions of the ballad.
Although it is tempting to explore the connection between Breton France
and Celtic Britain, it is more likely that this Louisiana French variant was
translated from American sources. Though many early British and Scottish
versions describe the coast in question as the "banks of Italy," an American
version published in Philadelphia in 1858 mentions "the banks of the Old
Tennessee," as does the Louisiana French version:

'J'ai marié un ouvrier, moi qui étais si vaillante fille,
Mais c'était de m'en dispenser sans attraper des reproches.'

'Mais quitte ton ouvrier, et viens t'en donc, c'est avec moi.
O viens t'en donc, c'est avec moi, dessus l'écore du Tennessee.'

'Dessus l'écore du Tennessee, quoi-ce t'aurais pour m'entretenir?
Quoi-ce t'aurais pour m'entretenir dessus l'écore du Tennessee?'

'J'en ai de ces gros navires qui naviguent dessus l'eau
Et soi-disant pour t'opposer de travailler.'

Au bout de trois jours, trois jours et trois semaines,
O la belle se mit à pleurer l'ennui de sa famille.

'Ne pleure donc pas la belle, je t'achèterai une robe de soie jaune
Qu'elle soit mais la couleur de l'or et de l'argent."

'Je ne pleure non pas ton or, ni ton or ni ton argent,
Mais je pleure ma famille que j'ai laissé là-bas.'

'Je t'ai pas toujours dit, la belle, et quand ce batiment calerait,
O il aurait une carlet à plus jamais resourdre.'

'Dessus l'écore du Tennessee, t'embrasserais ton cher et petit bébé,
O tu l'embrasserais à plus jamais revoir.'

(Traditional, as sung by Lanese Vincent and Sidney Richard, Kaplan, 1934;
Lomax/AFS 27b1; Swallow 8003-2.)

At the turn of the century, Cajun music entered a highly creative period, which among other things combined song and instrumental music in the same performance. There was a tendency in European tradition to keep songs and instrumental music separate. Dance music was almost exclusively instrumental except for *danse rondes* which were sung with no instrumental accompaniment. European song tradition tended to be textually oriented. Ballads and folksongs were traditionally unaccompanied and sung for their content. In African tradition, music, singing and dancing were all inextricably related and this may have influenced the combination of singing and instrumental traditions in the nineteenth century, not only in Louisiana, but throughout the American melting pot. The result of this process in Cajun music was the development of new songs which combined the two traditions. Instrumental parts were added to old ballads and words were composed for fiddle tunes. And both contributed to a wide new repertoire of music for dancing.

By this time, Cajun music reflected the blend of cultures in South Louisiana. In Dennis McGee's version of the traditional "Valse du vacher," for example, the singer, whose name reflects Irish roots and whose facial features reflect American Indian origins, describes the loneliness of a cowboy's life in French to the tune of a European mazurka clearly influenced by the blues:

Malheureuse, j'attrape mon cable et mes éperons
Pour moi aller voir à mes bêtes.
Chaque fois je m'en vas, c'est malheureux de me voir.
M'en aller moi tout seul, ma chérie....

(Traditional, as sung by Dennis McGee, *The Early Recordings*, Morning Star 45002; reissues from earlier 78 recordings.)

In this formative period, some of the most influential musicians were the black Creoles who brought a strong, rural blues element into Cajun music. Musicians such as Adam Fontenot and Amédé Ardoin developed new ways of making music with the newly acquired accordion. Ardoin's innovative, syncopated style made him a favorite at both black and white dances, but it was his powerful and highly creative singing that attracted the attention of early recording scouts. He was among the first of a group of Louisiana French musicians to record, immediately following Joe Falcon's pioneering

"Allons à Lafayette" in 1928. These early recordings, which the black Creole singer and accordionist made with white Cajun fiddler Dennis McGee, were immensely popular and influential. In the 1930s, his style became increasingly introspective. Because he recorded alone in this later period, his creative genius was unbridled and he composed songs which quickly became part of the classical Cajun music repertoire. His percussive accordion style also influenced the parallel development of zydeco/zarico music, later refined by contemporary zydeco/zarico musicians like Clifton Chenier. Some of Ardoin's most important compositions include the "Eunice Two-step" (today called "Jolie Catin"), "La Valse à Abe" ("La Valse de quatre-vingt-dix-neuf ans"), "Tante Aline" ("Chère Alice"), "Blues de la prison" ("Two-step de la prison"), "La Valse à Austin Ardoin" ("La Valse de l'orphelin"), and "Madame Atchen" ("La Robe barrée"):

Malheureuse, quoi t'as fait, oui avec moi?
Tu me fais du mal chaque fois je te regarde, malheureuse.
Quoi t'as dit, mais chère Jouline, tu me fais de mal.
Quoi faire t'as fait, mais tout ça t'as fait si long avec moi?

Je vas m'en aller, je vas m'en aller, mais dans la maison,
Je vas m'en aller, mais dans la maison sans toi, Jouline.

Malheureuse, regardez donc, mais quoi t'as fait à ton petit coeur.
J'ai pas pu juger ton histoire rapport à toi.
Ta bonne histoire est aussi bonne que tes bonnes paroles.
Ça tu m'as dit, toi, Jouline, ça m'a fait du mal.

Chère Jouline, je suis pas sûr d'être capable de m'en aller,
C'est pour rester pour espérer que tu t'en reviens.

O Jouline, comment je vas faire, tu me fais du mal.
Je suis content pour toi, Jouline, toi, mon cher petit monde.
T'aurais pas dû de me dire ça, ami joli coeur.

Dis ton idée, je suis pas comme ça, toi, malheureuse.
Chaque fois je dis, oui, je vas rentourner, mais à la maison.
Mon coeur fait mal juste pour assez pour moi pleurer.

(As sung by Amédé Ardoin; *Louisiana Creole Music*, Old Timey 124;

reissues from earlier 78 recordings.)

In the early twentieth century, commercial recording companies like RCA Victor, Bluebird, Decca, Columbia, and Okeh began recording ethnic and regional music throughout America, not out of an altruistic sense of cultural preservation but out of a straightforward desire to make money. Very simply, these companies realized that members of ethnic communities across the country would only be tempted to buy their record players if there was music they wanted to hear on record. In South Louisiana, this effort captured the end of this formative period in the development of Cajun music. It also helped to fix these early texts. Although the singers usually improvised lyrics with each performance, these recordings sounded the same each time they were played. Consequently, they came to be considered the standard versions.

Many of the first songs recorded were based on earlier tunes, but were themselves brand new adaptations. The first record to be released included Joe and Cléoma Falcon's "Allons à Lafayette" and "La Valse qui m'a porté en terre." "Allons à Lafayette," a two-step, was typical of the changes of the times, being a relatively new song adapted from an older tune, "Jeunes gens de la campagne."

Allons à Lafayette, mais pour changer ton nom.
On va t'appeller Madame, Madame Canaille Comeaux/comme moi.
Petite, t'est trop mignonne pour faire ta criminelle.
Comment tu crois, mais moi, je peux faire, mais moi tout seul.
Mais toi, mais joli coeur, regarde donc mais quoi t'as fait.
Si loin que moi, je suis de toi, mais ça, ça me fait pitié...

(As sung by Joe Falcon, *Louisiana Cajun Music,* vol. 1, Old Timey 108; reissues of early 78 recordings.)

Fiddlers such as Dennis McGee and Sady Courville, Ernest Frugé, the Connors, the Aguillards, and the Walkers still composed tunes, but the accordion was rapidly becoming the mainstay of traditional dance bands. Limited in notes and keys, it simplified Cajun music as songs that it could not play tended to fade from the scene. Fiddlers were often relegated to playing a duet accompaniment or a percussive second line below the dominant accordion's melody lead. The traditional instrumentation of the classic Cajun music group came to be the accordion, the fiddle, and the guitar, with sometimes a percussionist playing a triangle or some improvised instrumental noisemakers like spoons, bottles or a corrugated washboard.

Until the turn of the twentieth century, there was a wide variety of dance styles which included Old World waltzes, contredanses, *varsoviennes,* polkas, mazurkas, and cotillions, as well as two-steps, one-steps, *baisse-bas, la-las,* and breakdowns developed to accompany the contemporary musical styles. The simplification of musical styles brought on in part by modernization and the accordion simplified dance styles as well, leaving the waltz and the two-step as the major steps.

During this period, new songs were composed often utilizing ancient themes from French and African traditions. "Les Barres de la prison," by Canray Fontenot's classic blues waltz based on Douglas Bellard's original recording of "La Valse de la prison," for example, is a traditional gallows blues lament or prisoner's farewell which recalls the old French "Chanson de Mandrin."

> Good-bye, chère vieille mam,
> Good-bye, pauvre vieux pap,
> Good-bye à mes frères
> Et mes chères petites soeurs.
> Moi, j'ai été condamné
> Pour la balance de ma vie
> Dans les barres de la prison.
>
> Moi, j'ai roulé.
> Je m'ai mis à malfaire.
> J'avais la tête dure.
> J'ai rentré dans le tracas.
> Asteur je suis condamné
> Pour la balance de ma vie
> Dans les barres de la prison.
>
> Ma pauvre vieille maman,
> Elle s'a mis sur ses genoux,
> Les deux mains sur la tête,
> En pleurant pour moi.
> Elle dit, 'Mmmmmmmmm,
> Cher petit garçon,

Moi, je vas jamais te revoir.
Toi, t'as été condamné
Pour la balance de ta vie
Dans les barres de la prison.'

J'ai dit, 'Chère vieille maman,
Pleure pas pour moi.
Il faut tu pries pour ton enfant
Pour essayer de sauver son âme
De les flammes de l'enfer.'

(As sung by Canray Fontenot; *Bois sec: La Musique Créole;* Arhoolie 1070.)

In 1934, Lomax had recorded several unaccompanied ballads which used this theme. Compare the following:

Tu vas souffert, petite fille,
Pour ça t'après faire,
T'auras jamais de bonheur dans ta vie.
Oui, jour aujourd'hui,
Ma chère vieille maman
Dans la porte de la prison,
Les deux mains sur la tête, chère,
Pleurant pour moi.
O j'ai dit, 'Ma maman,
Pleure pas pour moi.
Demande à tes amis pour t'aider
Faire des prières pour sauver mon âme
De les flammes de l'enfer.
O voir aujourd'hui, voir aujourd'hui,
J'ai fini de te voir sur la terre du Bon Dieu.
Good-bye, petite fille, good-bye, petite fille,
Pour tous mes jours et tous tes tiens.'
J'ai dit, 'Fais dire aujourd'hui
Que j'après m'en aller.
Je pars, tu connais.'

Dit, 'Mon cher monde, garde-le voir..."

(From"Blues de Prison;" traditional, as sung by Joseph Jones, Jennings, 1934; Lomax/AFS 80a1; Swallow 8003-2.)

The following song, a remarkable version of the prisoner's lament based on a conversation between the prisoner and his mother and grandfather, utilizes another ancient motif, the keys to the cell. A similar ballad from French Canada, "Le Prisonnier et la fille du geôlier" (in Marius Barbeau's Folk Songs of French Canada), describes a jailer's daughter who falls in love with a prisoner and steals the prison keys to free him. He refuses to leave, choosing instead to accept his fate to be hanged. In this Louisiana version, the prisoner eventually is resigned to his fate and makes arrangements for his burial.

Chère Mam, o viens me donner les clefs,
Les clefs de la prison, les clefs de la prison.
'Baptiste, comment tu veux je te donne
Les clefs de la prison quand les officiers
Les ont accrochées dans le cou, les ont accrochées dans le cou.'

Chère Mam, ils vont venir me chercher,
Mais à neuf heures à soir,
Mais oui, c'est pour me pendre,
Mais à dix heures en nuit, mais à dix heures en nuit.

Chère Mam, c'est ça qui me fait plus de peine,
C'est de savoir ma mort,
Aussi longtemps d'avance, aussi longtemps d'avance.

Grandpère, mais qui s'a mis à genoux
En s'arrachant les cheveux, en s'arrachant les cheveux.
'Baptiste, comment t'as pu quitté,
Mais c'est pour t'en aller
Dans une si grande prison?'

Cher Pap, comment tu voulais je fais
Quand les officiers étaient tout le tour de moi
Avec les carabines, avec les carabines?

Chère Mam, c'est ça qui me fait plus de peine,
C'est de savoir ma mort
Aussi longtemps d'avance, aussi longtemps d'avance.

O Mam, ils vont venir me chercher,
Mais à neuf heurs à soir,
Mais oui, c'est pour me pendre,
Mais à dix heures en nuit, mais à dix heures en nuit.

Chère Mam, oui, je veux c'est toi qui m'emmènes,
Mais oui, mon corps en terre
Avec mon beau cheval cannel
Et ma belle voiture noire
Avec les quatre roues rouges, avec les quatres roues rouges.

(Traditional, as sung by Elita Hoffpauir, New Iberia, 1934; Lomax/AFS 31a2; Swallow 8003-2.)

This theme of the prisoner's farewell has recurred in many songs of the Cajun repertoire, including Amédé Ardoin's and Austin Pitre's versions of "Les Blues de la prison" and the ubiquitous "Les Flammes d'enfer."

Musicians continued to enlarge the repertoire, recording recently developed songs into the mid-1930s. By the time record companies began recording Cajun music, much of what could now be called the core repertoire already existed. "Jolie Blonde" was first recorded in 1928 by Joe Falcon's brothers-in-law, Amédé, Ophé and Cléopha Breaux. The principal elements of this classic Cajun waltz are already evident in this early version, then entitled "Ma Blonde est partie." The instrumentation was to become standard: accordion lead, fiddle and guitar accompaniment and a high-pitched singing style. The now-familiar themes of unfaithfulness and lost love are already important.

Jolie blonde, regardez donc quoi t'as fait,
Tu m'as quitté pour t'en aller.
Pour t'en aller avec un autre, oui, que moi,
Quel espoir et quel avenir, mais, moi, je vas avoir?

Jolie blonde, tu m'as laissé, moi tout seul,
Pour t'en aller chez ta famille.
Si t'aurais pas écouté tout les conseils des autres
Tu serais icitte avec moi aujourd'hui.

Jolie blonde, tu croyais il y avait juste toi,
Il y a pas juste toi dans le pays pour moi aimer.
Si je peux trouver juste une autre, jolie blonde,
Bon Dieu sait, moi, j'ai un tas.

(As sung by Amédé Breaux; *Louisiana Cajun Music,* vol. 5, Old Timey
114; reissues of earlier 78 recordings.)

   Mayeus Lafleur and Leo Soileau recorded "Hé Mam," and "La Valse
criminelle" before Lafleur's untimely death in 1929. Dennis McGee recorded
reels, breakdowns and bluesy waltzes with his brother-in-law Sady Courville
that same year. He also recorded several sides with Amédé Ardoin, flying
directly in the face of the strict segregationist codes of the times. Musicians
who would be important later in the revival of Cajun music after World War
II were already active. Lawrence Walker recorded several sides with his father
and uncle as the Walker Brothers. Nathan Abshire was already experimenting
with his combination of Cajun and blues traditions. Angelas LeJeune
recorded songs such as "La Valse de la Pointe Noire" (later known as the
"Kaplan Waltz") and "Bayou Pom-Pom" in the early 1930s. The recordings
of these and others like Moise Robin, the Segura Brothers and Blind Uncle
Gaspard were regional successes as Cajuns began to acquire record players.
   The advent of the radio further enhanced the popularity of certain
performers who had the good fortune to have access to the broadcast media.
Like the phonograph, radio, which broadcasted records and live
performances, lent importance to the most popular trends. It also introduced
into South Louisiana music from the music centers emerging in Nashville,
New York, and the West Coast.
   The early surge of musical creativity carried over into this new period as
Cajun performers adapted tunes they heard on the radio. Joseph and Cléoma
Falcon's "Les Filles à 'n oncle Hélaire" was a spicy syncopated tune with a
Caribbean-inspired beat. Some performers translated popular country hits
into French or composed new words to popular tunes to produce new songs
for the repertoire. Joe and Cléoma soon began including their own French
translations of American popular tunes like the Carter Family's "I'm

Joseph and Cléoma Falcon, ca. 1928.
(Photo courtesy of Ann Savoy,
from *Cajun Music: A Reflection of a People.*)

Amédé Ardoin, at his first communion.
(Photo courtesy of André Gladu, Pierre Daigle,
and Martin LeClerc.)

The Hackberry Ramblers, ca. 1940.
(Photo courtesy of Ann Savoy from *Cajun Music: A Reflection of a People*.)

Left:
Lawrence
Walker,
1950s.
(Photo
courtesy
La Louisianne
Records
and
Ann
Savoy.)

Above: Iry LeJeune and his band, 1950s. (Photo courtesy of
Eddie Shuler and Ann Savoy, from *Cajun Music: A Reflection of a People.*)

Below: Aldus Roger and the Lafayette Playboys, 1960.
(Phto courtesy of Ann Savoy, from *Cajun Music: A Reflection of a People.*)

Nathan Abshire performing at the first Tribute to Cajun Music Festival, Lafayette, Louisiana, 1974.   (Photo by Philip Gould.)

Canray Fontenot and Dewey Balfa.
(Photo by Philip Gould)

Curtis Corbello performing at the Tribute to Cajun Music Festival,
Lafayette, Louisiana 1978. (Photo by James Edmunds.)

Michael Doucet and Dennis McGee, in Louisiana French Folk Music class
at University of Southwestern Louisiana, 1979. (Photo by Philip Gould.)

Zachary Richard at the Tribute to Cajun Music Festival,
Lafayette, Louisiana, 1975. (Photo by Philip Gould)

Wayne Toups, on tour in Central and South America, 1987.
(Photo courtesy of Wayne Toups and U.S.I.A.)

Thinking Tonight of My Blue Eyes" and "Lu Lu's Back in Town" (Lulu est revenue dans village").

Leo Soileau, who accompanied Mayus Lafleur on the second Cajun record to be released formed one of the first string bands as the accordion began to lose favor during the 1930s. His Three Aces recorded early country and swing tunes, some translated, some not. His "Dans ton coeur tu aimes un autre" was a thinly disguised translation of the traditional "Columbus Stockade Blues." "Personne m'aime pas" was a French takeoff on the popular song, "Nobody's Darling But Mine."

By the mid-1930s, Cajuns were reluctantly, though inevitably, becoming Americanized. America, caught in the "melting pot" ideology, tried to homogenize its diverse ethnic and cultural elements. At the national level, America had fought in a major war which for the first time in a century divided most of the world into camps. National leaders like Teddy Roosevelt felt that there was a danger that this country, which was built of people from all over the world, might blow apart itself. Roosevelt insisted that there was no such thing as a "hyphenated American" and urged members of various ethnic and national groups to conform to America or to leave it.

Part of this conformity included learning English, for Roosevelt insisted that there was "room for but one language in this country and that is the English language, for we must assure that the crucible produces Americans and not some random dwellers in a polyglot boardinghouse." The French language, native to the Cajuns and their music, was banned from schools throughout South Louisiana as a result of state board of education policy in 1916. This action was confirmed by the new state constitution of 1921 which stripped the French language of its historical official status. Speaking French was not only against the rules, it became increasingly unpopular as Cajuns attempted to escape the stigma attached to their culture.

In the 1930s the efforts of another Roosevelt to ease the national pain of Great Depression brought more changes to South Louisiana. Work projects brought a generation of young Cajuns out into the rest of America. A new money-based economy brought the Cajuns into the marketplace where they needed to speak English to do business with America. The new highways and bridges built by Huey Long and improved transportation opened previously isolated areas to the rest of the country. Money from the budding oil industry brought the sons of sharecroppers off the farm and into the industrial workplace. With regular paychecks for the first time in the history of their families, many Cajuns were able to afford modern conveniences such as refrigerators and radios which diminished the need for traditional gatherings like *boucheries* and house dances. They also bought automobiles which allowed them to extend their sphere of activity.

The Cajuns had always learned from their neighbors and their neighbors from them. Now, however, the immigration of Anglo-American outsiders to Cajun country was too much too fast. The newcomers were no longer motivated to learn the native language and the culture of the land. At the same time, the Cajuns' understanding of the world was greatly enlarged, making them seek to learn the ways of the land in the larger context of America. The Americanization of the Cajuns was finally underway in earnest.

These social and cultural changes of the 1930s and 1940s were clearly reflected in the recorded music of the period. The slick programming on the radio and later television inadvertently undermined the comparatively unpolished traditional sounds and forced them underground. The previously dominant accordion, for example, faded completely from the popular scene, partly because the old-style music had lost popularity and partly because the instruments, hitherto manufactured in Germany, were unavailable.

As the western-swing and bluegrass sounds from Texas and Tennessee swept the country, string bands which imitated the music of Bob Wills and the Texas Playboys and copied Bill Monroe's high lonesome sound sprouted across South Louisiana. Among the early leaders in this new trend were the Hackberry Ramblers (with Luderin Darbonne on fiddle who recorded new, lilting versions of what had begun to emerge as the classic Cajun repertoire, such as "Jolie Blonde." They also performed new compositions such as "Une Piastre ici, une piastre là-bas," a song which shows what it means to live in a money-based economy caught in the throes of the Great Depression:

> Quand j'ai eu vingt et un ans
> Mon père m'a dit que j'étais dedans.
>
> C'est l'heure que t'arrêtes de dépenser
> Une piastre ici, une piastre là-bas...'

(From "Une Piastre ici, une piastre là-bas," as performed by the Hackberry Ramblers; *Louisiana Cajun Music,* vol. 3, Old Timey 110; reissues from earlier 78 recordings.)

Freed from the limitations imposed by the accordion, string bands readily absorbed various outside influences. Darbonne's Ramblers were the first to use electrical amplification systems. Dancers across South Louisiana were shocked in the mid-1930s to hear music which came not only from the bandstand, but also from the opposite end of the dance hall through speakers. In places not yet reached by the rural electrification project (REA), these early sound systems were powered by a Model T idling behind the building. The electric steel guitar eventually replaced the acoustic dobro or National steel guitar, and trap drums were added to the standard instrumentation as Cajuns continued to experiment with new sounds borrowed from Anglo-American musicians.

An important stylistic change occurred in the fiddle music component of Cajun music. Amplification made it unnecessary for fiddlers to bear down with the bow in order to be heard; therefore, many developed a lighter, lilting touch, producing an airier, almost glib sound which was quite different from the intense, mournful earlier styles. Cajun fiddlers, being influenced by Anglo-American string bands, began to include bits of the repertoire of those groups in their performances, including songs like "The Maiden's Prayer" and "The Ranger's Waltz," lively, fancy fiddling tunes like "Ragtime Annie" and "Down South," and popular radio tunes like "If You Don't See Your Mama Every Night" and "Kentucky."

Undoubtedly the most popular Cajun musician of his day, Harry Choates was born near Rayne, in Acadia Parish, but as with so many of his countrymen, he moved to East Texas in the 1940s with his family to work in ship building and in the oil fields. This move greatly influenced his music. In songs such as the "Austin Special," "Grand Texas," and the "Port Arthur Blues," he helped to develop the *"tu m'as quitté pour t'en aller au Grand Texas"* theme which was to become ubiquitous in modern Cajun music. Choates also sprinkled his songs, like "Louisiana Boogie," with English terms to reach a larger audience:

Tu m'as quitté pour t'en aller,
Pour t'en aller, mais chère, si loin,
C'est pour faire le boogie-woogie,
Faire le boogie-woogie,
Après faire le boogie-woogie.
Je connais ça sera pas pour longtemps.

Tu honky-tonk ici, tu honky-tonk là-bas,

Tu honky-tonk, tu honky-tonk, tu honky-tonk tout le temps.
T'es après faire le boogie-woogie,
Après faire le boogie-woogie
Après faire le boogie-woogie.
Je connais ça sera pas pour longtemps...

(From *Harry Choates,* Arhoolie 5027; reissues of earlier 78 recordings.)

His popularity carried him as far west as Austin, in the heart of Anglo-Texas, on regular weekend dance jobs. His simplified interpretations of older Cajun standards such as "Jolie Blonde" and "Pauvre Hobo" were regional hits, even attracting some regional attention, and became the standard versions performed by bands throughout South Louisiana. He also recorded many country fiddle standards like "Rubber Dolly."

Other bands recorded bilingual songs, reflecting a gradual gravitation toward the English language. In the late 1940s, for example, a Cajun group ironically called the Oklahoma Tornadoes released "Dans la prison":

Well, I left for Louisiana about a year ago,
Going to Texas, travelling with a show.
I landed in old Houston doing mighty fine,
Until I met that woman, and now I'm doing time.

Dans la prison, la hell avec ça.
Moi, je connais ça sera longtemps.
Dans la prison, la hell avec ça.
Moi, je m'en reviens dans vingt-quatre ans . . .

(From *Louisiana Cajun Music,* vol. 4; Old Timey 111; reissues of earlier 78 recordings.)

Darbonne's group, which had recorded French swing tunes as the Hackberry Ramblers, recorded English country tunes as the Riverside Ramblers (a name they acquired when their radio show was sponsored by Montgomery Ward's Riverside tires). This version of the group featured the singing of Joe Werner on regional hits such as "Wondering" (which predated Webb Pierce's national hit by a few years). The transition was nearly complete; recorded Cajun music showed increasing discomfort with the French language and traditional sounds. Even Joe Falcon's wife Cléoma had joined the move away from the roots, recording a version of "Hand Me Down My Walking Cane" entirely in English.

By the late 1940s, the music recorded by commercial companies signalled an unmistakable tendency toward Americanization. Yet, there persisted an undercurrent of traditional music. The accordion, for example, completely absent from popular recordings during this period, was played on back porches and for family and friends at house dances and on holidays. Older songs were preserved in the memories of those who continued to hum, whistle, and sing them informally. This traditional foundation would resurface first in the recordings of Iry LeJeune, a young accordion player and singer from the Pointe Noire area south of Church Point, in Acadia Parish. Greatly influenced by the earlier recordings of Amédé Ardoin and by the music of his own uncles and cousins, among them Angelas and Steven LeJeune, he tagged along with Virgil Bozman's Oklahoma Tornadoes in 1948 to record "La Valse du Pont d'Amour," in the intensely soulful turn-of-the-century style and in French.

Hé, petite fille,
Moi, je me vois
Après partir
Mais m'en aller donc te rejoindre.
O chère petite fille,
Quand même tu voudrais
T'en revenir, petit monde,
Regarde donc, je veux plus te voir.

Hé, tu m'as dit,
Petite fille, criminelle,
Tu sais toi, tu voulais plus
M'aimer malheureuse.
Tu connais, petite fille,
Que moi, j'ai pris ça dur,
Pris ça assez dur
Que moi, j'ai pris les grands chemins...

(©Iry LeJeune and Eddie Shuler, "La Valse du Pont d'Amour," from *Iry LeJeune: The Greatest,* vol. 2, Goldband 7741, reissues of earlier recordings; TEK Publishing, all rights reserved, used by permission.)

Skeptics wondered at his forsaking current trends, but the recording, an unexpected success, presaged a revival of the earlier styles. Iry LeJeune became a pivotal figure in a revival fueled by the return of homesick GIs seeking to soothe their *mal de pays* in a hot, cultural bath. All over the country, soldiers wanted to eat home cooking. In South Louisiana that meant rice and gravy and gumbo, no more potatoes. And they wanted to hear homemade music. In South Louisiana, that meant Cajun music, no more Hit Parade for a while. These soldiers literally populated the dance halls where they drank and danced to forget the horrors of the war. Dance halls which provided traditional music flourished, and musicians such as Lawrence Walker, Austin Pitre, and Nathan Abshire brought their abandoned accordions out of the closet and once again recorded old-style Cajun music.

The musicians who helped to revive Cajun music in the late 1940s and early 1950s were not only historically important. They were also fine performers and folk poets. The revival of the 1950s consequently produced a corpus of new songs to go along with the retooled traditional sounds. Iry Lejeune adapted many older Amédé Ardoin songs, preserving some elements, such as Ardoin's symbolic mistress Joline, while adding new words and tightening the lyrics. Often working with his friend and producer Eddie Shuler, he also composed a few memorable songs of his own, including "Grand Bosco" and "J'ai fait une grosse erreur."

Quand j'ai quitté de la maison,
Moi, je croyais j'avais raison.
J'avais dit que j'aurais jamais revenu.
Ça a pas été si longtemps,
Je t'ai eu de besoin à mon côté.
C'est là j'ai vu que j'avais fait une grosse erreur.

Quand je t'ai rejoint dessus la rue
Avec un autre à ton côté,
Tu ressemblais si contente et aussi heureuse.
Avec des larmes dedans mes yeux
Et mon cher cœur aussi cassé,
Moi, je savais j'avais fait une grosse erreur.

Dans la clarté du soleil
Et la lumière de la lune,
Moi, j'ai vu personne était si heureux.

Avec des larmes dans mes yeux
Et mon cher cœur aussi cassé,
C'est là j'ai vu j'avais fait une grosse erreur.

("J'ai fait une grosse erreur," as performed by Iry LeJeune, on *The Legendary Iry LeJeune,* vol. 1, Goldband 7740.)

As a bandleader, Lawrence Walker was a perfectionist. He carefully controlled and crafted the sound of his Wandering Aces band. He was also a gifted singer and composed several Cajun music classics, including "Petits yeux noirs" and the "Reno Waltz." In his "Chère Alice," Walker gave a final form to the story-song about the ill-fated love between Alice Royer and petit Dom Hanks. His "Valse du malchanceux" demonstrates Walker's solid sense of oral poetics.

C'est ça la valse moi, j'appelle la valse du malchanceux.
C'est ça la valse qui jouait tant dans le temps que je courtisais.
C'est ça la valse qu'était après jouer le soir je l'ai demandée.
C'est ça la valse qu'était après jouer quand son papa me l'a refusée.

C'est ça la valse qu'était après jouer le soir que je l'ai volée.
C'est ça la valse qu'était après jouer quand ils m'ont trouvé.
C'est ça la valse qu'était après jouer quand ils m'ont fait la marier.
C'est ça la valse qu'était après jouer quand on s'a séparé.

C'est ça la valse je veux Dick me joue sur le lit de ma mort.
C'est ça la valse je veux Dick me joue le soir que je vas mourir.
C'est ça la valse je veux Dick me joue jusqu'à la porte du cimetière.
C'est ça la valse moi, j'appelle la valse du malchanceux.

(©Lawrence Walker, "La Valse du malchanceux," on *The Late, Great Lawrence Walker,* La Louisianne 126; La Lou Publishing, all rights reserved, used by permission.)

Nathan Abshire was also influenced by Amédé Ardoin, though more in style than content. Many of his compositions contain a key word which reflects the major characteristic of his music: "Service Blues," "French

Blues," "Popcorn Blues," "Offshore Blues," and his signature song, the
"Pine Grove Blues:"

> Hé négresse, ayoù t'as été hier au soir, ma négresse?
> (J'ai été au village.)
> Hé négresse, ayoù t'as été hier au soir, ma négresse?
> (J'ai été au village et je m'ai saoulé.)
> T'as revenu à ce matin. Le soleil était après se lever.
> Ça me fait de la peine pour toi.
>
> Hé négresse, ayoù t'as passé hier au soir, ma négresse?
> (J'ai passé dans la barrière.)
> Hé négresse, ayoù t'as passé hier au soir, ma négresse?
> (J'ai passé dans la barrière. J'étais après me sauver.)
> T'as revenu à ce matin. Ta robe était toute déchirée.
> Ça me fait de la peine pour toi.

Another composer of the post-war revival period, Shirley Bergeron created
several beautiful songs, including "La Valse de la belle," the "Old Home
Waltz," and "Quelle étoile." Other Cajun singers may have been intimidated
by Bergeron's soaring high-pitched vocals; few of his songs entered into the
standard dance band repertoire despite their moving storylines. His "J'ai fait
mon idée" is typical of the poetics of dance band lyrics: brief,
impressionistic, and only suggestive, as compared to the longer, more
narrative treatment in other forms such as the ballad, or in the legends or
tales of spoken tradition.

> J'ai fait mon idée en faisant mon paquet.
> Ta bonne vieille maman, elle s'a mis à pleurer.
> Elle m'a dit, "Quoi faire toi, t'es comme ça?"
> Moi, j'ai répondu, "Moi, j'ai fait mon idée."
>
> Les enfants sont donnés. Leurs papiers sont signés.
> Ça qui me fait du mal, c'est qu'ils vont m'oublier.

Il a cassé notre ménage. C'est ça qui me décourage.
C'est pour ça moi, je te dis, "Moi, j'ai fait mon idée."

(©Shirley Bergeron, "J"ai fait mon idée," on *The Sounds of Cajun Music*,
Lanor 1000; Jon Music, all rights reserved, used by permission.)

In the 1950s, a few musicians, such as Joe Bonsall and Rodney Lejeune,
whose families had moved to Texas to work in the oil fields and shipyards,
set up bands and began playing Cajun music across the Sabine River in
what became known as Cajun Lapland (where Cajun culture laps over into
Texas). Local recording pioneers such as George Khoury, Eddie Shuler, J.
D. Miller, and later, Floyd Soileau and Carol Rachou, picked up the slack
left by the national producers who by then had turned exclusively to widely
marketable performers. Though bearing the marks of Americanization,
Cajun music was making a dramatic comeback just as interest in the culture
and language quickened before the 1955 Acadian bicentennial celebration, led
by politicians like Dudley J. LeBlanc and Roy Theriot.

In the early 1950s, many dance bands performed as often as seven and
eight times a week. Some of these groups developed a tight, well-
orchestrated, dance-band style, keeping the successive eight or sixteen bar
instrumental rides learned from swing and bluegrass music. (The typical
pattern of instrumental rides which developed in Cajun music was:
accordion lead, accordion break, vocal lead, steel guitar shuffle, fiddle break,
fiddle lead, accordion break, accordion lead.) Groups incorporated palatable
elements from various new styles, including early rock-and-roll, to develop
new sounds.

Even the names of many of these revived groups reflected the enduring
influence of their brush with Americanization. Lawrence Walker's group
was called the Wandering Aces. Austin Pitre's was the Evangeline
Playboys, after their native Evangeline Parish. Nathan Abshire called his
band the Pine Grove Boys, after their regional hit, the "The Pine Grove
Blues."

Some began performing on local radio stations; others, such as Aldus
Roger and the Lafayette Playboys and Happy Fats and the Mariné Band,
were even featured on area television. Most bands were composed of
musicians who made a living from other regular jobs, but a few, such as
Jimmy C. Newman and Doug Kershaw, became professionals who only
played music for a livelihood. They quickly realized that the Louisiana
French market was limited and felt they would have to perform in English if

they were to attract an audience large enough to support them. Newman continued to sing a few of his native Cajun songs after he moved from Mamou to Nashville, but his direction was clearly toward American country music. He became a regular on the Grand Old Opry with hits such as "Cry, Cry, Darling" (#9 in May 1954) and "A Fallen Star" (#42, June 1957). He eventually hit the country music charts with a few songs that played on Cajun themes such as "Alligator Man" (#22, December 1961), "Bayou Talk" (#12, December 1962), and "Boo Dan" (#31, May 1969). Kershaw recycled older Cajun tunes to produce new songs with English lyrics, like his "I'm Not Strong Enough," which is based on the ancient "Valse du bambocheur," his "Cajun Stripper," a souped-up version of the "Bosco Stomp," and his "Mama Rita in Hollywood," a revival of the traditional "J'ai été-z-au bal." Like Newman, Kershaw also performed original compositions in which he skillfully exploited his Cajun heritage, such as "Cajun Joe" and his best known hits, "Louisiana Man" (#10, February 1961) and "Diggy Liggy Lo" (#14, August 1961). Kershaw developed a small, national following, even appearing on the CBS television network's immensely popular "Ed Sullivan Show."

In the 1950s and '60s, South Louisiana, like the rest of the nation and much of the world, was affected by the emergence of what came to be called rock and roll. The sons and daughters of Cajun musicians followed the musical lead of fellow Louisiana musicians Jerry Lee Lewis and Antoine "Fats" Domino to produce what English author John Broven has called Swamp Pop. More a songwriter than a performer, Bobby Charles (Guidry) gave American popular culture a lasting line with his "See You Later, Alligator" (#30 on the rhythm and blues charts in 1955 and subsequently an international hit for Bill Haley and the Comets). He also wrote songs that became national hits for Clarence "Frogman" Henry ("But I Do") and Fats Domino ("Four Winds," "Walking to New Orleans," and "Before I Grow Too Old"). Within the region, bands with names like Bobby Page (Elwood Dugas) and the Riff Raffs and Clint West (Clinton Guillory) and the Boogie Kings, recorded songs that made the local hit parade. A few South Louisiana musicians even affected the national pop music scene: Warren Storm (Shexnayder), "Prisoner's Song" (#81, August 1958), Cookie (Huey Thierry) and the Cupcakes, "Mathilda" (#47, January 1959), Rod Bernard and the Twisters, "This Should Go On Forever" (#20, March 1959), Johnny Preston (Courville), "Running Bear" (#10, October 1959), among others. Dale (Houston) and Grace (Broussard) reached #1 on the charts with "I'm Leaving It Up to You" (October 1963).

Country music and swamp pop were tempting alternatives and Cajun music was again straying far afield from its traditional sources. Deliberate efforts would be necessary, in Dewey Balfa's words, "to water the roots so that the tree would not die."

The needed impulse came from the national level. Alan Lomax, a member of the Newport Folk Foundation, had become interested in Cajun and Creole music while collecting, in the 1930s, traditional music across the country for the Library of Congress. In the manner prescribed by activist ethnomusicologist Charles Seeger, Lomax sent "cultural guided missles" to document and encourage the preservation of the music during the 1950s. While a professor of English at Louisiana State University in Baton Rouge, Harry Oster recorded a musical spectrum which ranged from unaccompanied ballads to contemporary dance tunes, especially in Evangeline and Vermilion parishes. His collection, which stressed the evolution of Cajun music, attracted the attention of local activists like Paul Tate and Revon Reed.

The work of Harry Oster and Alan Lomax caught the imagination of the Newport group, and fieldworkers Ralph Rinzler and Mike Seeger were sent to find Cajun musicians for the festival. Cajun dance bands had played at the National Folk Festival as early as the 1930s (when Lawrence Walker accompanied the Broussard family band to the festival in Dallas), but little echo of these performances reached Louisiana. Rinzler and Seeger, seeking the gutsy roots of Cajun music, invited Gladius Thibodeaux, Louis "Vinesse" LeJeune (a cousin of Iry), and Dewey Balfa to represent Louisiana at the 1964 Newport Folk Festival. There alongside nationally known folk revivalists like Joan Baez, Peter, Paul and Mary, and Bob Dylan, they performed the turn-of-the-century, unamplified music which made the Louisiana cultural establishment uneasy. These "unrefined" sounds embarrassed the upwardly mobile "genteel Acadians" who barely tolerated the more polished sounds of popular dance bands like Belton Richard and the Musical Aces. They considered the music chosen for the Newport Festival crude, "nothing but chanky-chank." An editorial by Burton Grindstaff in the Opelousas *Daily World* (October 20, 1965) unabashedly illustrated this sentiment:

> Cajuns brought some mighty fine things down from Nova Scotia with them, including their jolly selves, but their so-called music is one thing I wish they hadn't.

The first time my sensitive ears were shattered by the dissonant squall of a Cajun musician was in Eunice back in 1946. I was told that an acquaintance of mine, a fellow who seemed to be normal in other respects, was going to play an accordion 'Cajun style' at some kind of local program. I was foolish enough to look forward to the event, and even to think I might be in on the discovery of something great that had been hidden from the rest of the country all these years. I broke through a window after the first stanza, went home and doused my head in a bucket of water to drown out the sound...

Grindstaff ended his column with a prediction:

I suppose there will be no containing them if they get a really bad needle on one of those records the Newport festival people took back with them and some of these modern folk music people get an earful.

All we can do is sit back and wait for the verdict from Newport, scared stiff. I am not sure Cajun music is on trial in Newport. It may be us. Their verdict could subject us to tortures like the world has never known before.

This remarkable tirade was a fairly accurate assessment of the opinion of a certain class of Cajuns and Creoles. Despite Mr. Grindstaff's grim predictions, however, the Newport organizers were intent on showing the beauty and impact of root music. Their instinct proved well-founded as huge crowds gave the old-time music standing ovations. Two members of the Louisiana group were simply impressed. The third was Dewey Balfa, a fiddler and vocalist in a family band called The Musical Brothers who had accompanied Thibodeaux and LeJeune as a last-minute replacement on guitar. He was so moved by the experience that he returned to Louisiana determined "to bring home the echo of the standing ovation" they had received at the Newport Festival.

Dewey began working on a small scale, among his friends and family in Mamou, Basile and Eunice. Rinzler, who continued his fieldwork through the 1960s, recognized Dewey's budding activism and urged him on. The Newport Folk Festival, under the guidance of Lomax, routed money and fieldworkers into the area through the newly established Louisiana Folk Foundation. Other groups were invited to perform at Newport, including black Creoles (Alphonse Ardoin and Canray Fontenot) as well as Cajuns (Adam and Cyprien Landreneau). Financial support and outside approval brought about gradual changes on the inside. Local activists such as Paul Tate, Revon Reed, Catherine and Edward Blanchet, Milton and Patricia Rickels became involved in preserving the music, language, and culture. Dewey Balfa did not have the educational base of these members of the foundation, but his innate command of the material more than made up for this deficiency, and his clear sense of mission made him an invaluable member of this task force.

With the help of the Newport Folk Festival Foundation, this group organized traditional contests at local events such as the Abbeville Dairy Festival, the Opelousas Yambilee, and the Crowley Rice Festival. Special concerts were presented so that people would have an opportunity to listen to their music without the distractions of a smoke-filled dance hall.

Eventually Dewey convinced Swallow Records, a local company, to release a recording of traditional Cajun music alongside its more modern listings. Superbly performed ancient songs like "La Valse du bambocheur" and "Parlez-nous à boire" which had attracted Rinzler's attention to the Balfa Brothers sound, also proved popular among the heritage-minded Cajuns of the late 1960s, and led to subsequent albums on Swallow and other labels, including Arhoolie (from California), Rounder (Massachusetts), Folkways (New York), Expression Spontanée (France), and Sonet (England). One of the Balfa Brothers' most important contributions was to set the example of looking back to recycle the best of the traditional material. In this effort, they sometimes composed new words for old tunes, such as Will's "Valse de Balfa," a remarkable testimony to undying love.

Quand j'ai parti de la maison,
J'avais fait mon idée.
J'étais parti pour te chercher, chère,
Ou mourir au bout de mon sang.

Quand j'ai arrivé à ta maison,
J'en ai trouvé un autre avec toi.
Ça, ça a cassé mon cœur, chère,
J'aime mieux mourir que voir ça.

Si j'aurais cinq jours dans ma vie,
J'en donnerais trois dans les cinq
Pour passer les deux autres avec toi.
J'aimerais mourir dedans tes bras.

Soon other musicians began searching through their memories to revive old songs instead of only translating outside sources of new material.

In 1968, the state of Louisiana officially recognized the Cajun cultural revival which had been brewing under the leadership of certain musicians and political leaders such as Dewey Balfa and Dudley LeBlanc. In that year, it created the Council for the Development of French in Louisiana (CODOFIL) which, under the chairmanship of James Domengeaux, began its efforts on political, psychological and educational fronts to erase the stigma Louisianians had long attached to the French language and culture. The creation of French classes in elementary schools began to reverse the policy which had barred the language from the schoolgrounds.

Early in the development of CODOFIL's political strategy, Domengeaux had decided that his efforts should be concentrated in the classroom, explaining that if the language could be saved, the rest would follow. He quickly changed his approach, however, when he realized, as he later put it, "that language and culture are inseparable." Influenced by Rinzler and Balfa, CODOFIL organized a first Tribute to Cajun Music festival in 1974 with a three-hour concert designed to present an historical overview of Cajun music from its origins to modern styles. The echo of Newport had finally come home. Dewey Balfa's message of cultural self-esteem was heard by over 12,000 enthusiastic participants, and was heard again and again as the festival subsequently became an annual celebration of Cajun music and culture.

Dewey's message was complex and aimed in many directions at once. The festival not only provided exposure for the musicians but also presented them as cultural heroes and in the same motion made them available to the ones who needed them most. House dances had given way to public dance halls in the 1930s and, especially after Prohibition, only those eighteen years old and older were able to hear Cajun music with any regularity. Young people listened to what music they could hear, usually on records and radio. Festivals helped to close this cultural generation gap by giving young Cajuns the opportunity to hear the music of their heritage. Later, combination restaurant/dance halls such as Mulate's, Randol's, Préjean's and Bélizaire's reinforced the process. Since these dancehalls also served food, children were able to accompany their parents and grandparents to appreciate their music and learn their dances. Many young performers were attracted to the revalidated Cajun music scene and became interested in playing the music of their fathers and grandfathers. At the same time, local French movement officials observing from backstage realized the impact of the grassroots and began to stress the native Louisiana French culture in the revival of French in Louisiana.

Balfa's dogged pursuit of cultural recognition carried him further than he had ever expected. In 1977, he received a Folk Artist in the Schools grant from the National Endowment for the Arts through Atlanta's Southern Folk Revival project to bring his message into elementary school classrooms. He became a regular on the national folk festival touring circuit along with many of his colleagues. Balfa has given workshops in such places as the Smithsonian Institution and the Library of Congress. In 1982, he was presented with the National Heritage Award and in 1986 his album *Souvenirs* was nominated for a Grammy Award in the Ethnic Music category. In 1987, despite his protests that he had little formal education, Balfa was finally convinced to accept a temporary position to teach courses in Cajun music and culture at the University of California at Fresno. The following year, he was appointed Adjunct Professor of Cajun Music at the University of Southwestern Louisiana.

Cajun music seems likely to live for at least another generation. The renewed creativity within the tradition (as opposed to the simple imitation of outside styles) makes earlier predictions of imminent disintegration seem hasty. Camey Doucet has experimented widely with new songs and styles. Recent compositions by musicians such as D. L. Menard, Belton Richard and Ivy Dugas continue to enlarge the stock repertoire of contemporary dance bands. Menard's "La Porte d'en arrière," which almost immediately became an integral part of the standard repertoire when it was released in the early 1960s, reiterates the *l'enfant perdu* theme encountered in many Cajun songs, but treats it in a humorous vein. Members of his group, the Louisiana Aces, found this humorous treatment so unusual that they hesitated at first to record this classic.

Moi et la belle, on avait été-z-au bal,

On a passé dans tous les honky tonks.
On s'en a revenu le lendemain matin,
Le jour était après se casser.
J'ai passé dedans la porte d'en arrière.

Après-midi, moi, j'ai été-z-au village
Et je m'ai saoulé que je pouvais plus marcher.
Ils m'ont ramené back à la maison,
Il y avait de la compagnie, c'était du monde étranger.
J'ai passé dedans la porte d'en arrière.

Mon vieux père, un soir quand j'ai arrivé,
Il a essayé de changer mon idée.
Je l'ai pas écouté, moi, j'avais trop la tête dure.
'Un jour à venir, mon nègre, tu vas avoir du regret.
T'as passé dedans la porte d'en arrière.'

J'ai eu un tas d'amis tant que j'avais de l'argent.
Asteur j'ai plus d'argent, mais ils voulont plus me voir.
J'ai été dans le village et moi, je m'ai mis dans le tracas.
La loi m'a ramassé. Moi, je suis parti dans la prison.
On va passer dedans la porte d'en arrière.

Belton Richard's music represents a strong marriage of traditional and swamp pop styles. His translations of contemporary country and pop music hits, such as his versions of "Behind Closed Doors" ("En arrière des portes fermées") and "The Streak" ("La Petite Éclair"), have been successful on the French Louisiana market, but his songwriting abilities are demonstrated most clearly in his original compositions, such as "Le Paradis des musiciens," and "Un autre soir ennuyant."

Un autre soir ennuyant
Quand toi, t'es pas là.
Les larmes tombent dans mon cœur.
C'est ça qui me fait peur.
Un autre soir ennuyant.

Le soleil après se coucher
Et toi, t'es pas là.
Les étoiles après briller
Et moi, je suis après pleurer
Un autre soir ennuyant...

(©Belton Richard, from "Un autre soir ennuyant," on *Belton Richard and the Musical Aces: Modern Sounds in Cajun Music*, Swallow 6010; Flat Town Music, all rights reserved, used by permission.)

In addition to obvious translations of top-forty hits such as "Mauvais Leroy Brown," Ivy Dugas has also produced several contemporary Cajun classics, including "La Valse à Mam" and the self-consciously optimistic "Valse de l'Héritage."

Après essayer de préserver
Le langage des Cajuns,
Et la musique qu'on aimait,
Et nos petits écouter.
Mais tant qu'à pour moi,
C'est ici, mais pour rester.
J'étais Cadien quand j'ai été né,
Et je seras Cadien quand je vas mourir.

Sur l'île de la baie
Ils ont arrivé sur des bateaux.
À l'histoire à Évangeline
Elle a espéré sur son beau.
Ayoù le manger est si bon,
Et la religion est si forte.
J'étais Cadien quand j'ai été né,
Et je seras Cadien quand je vas mourir.

(©Ivy Dugas, "Valse de l'Héritage," on *Louisiana Cajun French Music Association: Laisse le bon temps rouler*, vol. 1, CFMA Records 02; Acadia Music, all rights reserved, used by permission.)

On the eastern side of the Atchafalaya Basin, the accordion was briefly popular but faded from the scene during the 1930s and 1940s and did not return after World War II as it did on the southwestern prairies. There is a French music style along Bayous Terrebonne and Lafourche, but it is highly influenced by country and rock sounds. The tradition of the *chansonnier* is especially strong in this region, as heard in the rich baritone voices of singers like Vin Bruce and L. J. Foret. Many songs are adapted from the English, like Vin Bruce's "La Prière de la jeune fille" ("The Maiden's Prayer"). Original compositions such as Bruce's "Dedans la Louisiane" and Foret's "Le Chemin des coeurs cassés" also have a distinct country flavor. Swamp pop performers like Joe Barry and Gene Rodrigue have provided a rock-influenced sound for the region as well.

Back on the southwestern prairies, young Cajuns, discovering local models besides country and rock stars, began performing the music of their heritage. Yet they did not reject modern sounds while adopting older ones. Zachary Richard's first Cajun music recordings reflected his brief flirtation with country sounds in songs like "Marcher le plancher:"

C'est pas les pillules qui m'empêchent de dormir.
Je suis après marcher le plancher avec des rêves doux de toi.

Ni lune, ni étoile va briller ce soir.
J'ai vidé la bouteille il y a assez longtemps.
J'ai marché des grands trous dans mes bottes de cowboy,
Après marcher le plancher avec des rêves doux de toi...

(©Zachary Richard, from "Marcher le plancher," on *Mardi Gras,* original issue on CBS, now only available in English version on RZ 1005; Marais Bouleur Music, all rights reserved, used by permission.)

He eventually brought rock and pop music trends, as well as additional lyrics, into his arrangements of traditional music, including "Travailler, c'est trop dur" and "L'Arbre est dans ses feuilles." Some of his original compositions, such as "Réveille," "Ballade de Beausoleil," and "Ma Louisiane," reflect the sense of history and cultural activism he encountered in Quebec and the Canadian Maritimes in the early part of his career.

La Louisiane, ma Louisiane,
C'est beau au printemps, c'est chaud en été.

C'est frais en automne, c'est trempe en hiver.
Moi, je suis fier d'être Cadien.

Oublie voir pas qu'on est Cadien,
Mais cher garçon, mais chère petite fille.
On était ici avant les Américains.
On sera ici après qu'ils sont partis.

Ton papa et ta maman étaient chassés de l'Acadie
Pour le grand craint d'être Français.
Mais ils ont trouvé un beau pays.
Merci bon Dieu pour la Louisiane.

(©Ralph Zachary Richard, from "Ma Louisiane," on *Mardi Gras,* RZ 1005; Marais Bouleur Music, all rights reserved, used by permission.)

Other songs, such as "Allons Danser" and "Antibone Legbo," show an influence from New Orleans music figures such as Fats Domino, Professor Longhair, Dr. John, and the Neville Brothers. Always the innovator, Richard has even developed Cajun reggae and Cajun rap. Overall, one of Richard's most important contributions was the discovery of new outlets. He found a way to support his career as a professional musician singing in French by reaching out to Quebec and France, where he has had several gold records.

Michael Doucet has incorporated rock, jazz and classical styles into the carefully researched traditional base of his group Beausoleil in songs such as ""Belle", "Je m'endors," "Les Barres de la prison" and "Contredanse de Mamou." He has composed new songs such as "Zydeco gris-gris" and "Hommage aux frères Balfa," arranged instrumental parts for previously unaccompanied songs such as "Pierrot Grouillet et Mademoiselle Josette," and "J'ai marié un ouvrier," and written new original words for traditional instrumentals such as "Le Gigue français," and "Johnnie peut pas danser:"

Pauvre petit Johnnic voudrait danser,
Mais pauvre petit Johnnie peut pas danser.
Il a essayé, il a essayé,
Mais pauvre petit Johnnie peut pas danser.

Tous les samedis soirs, mais dans la soirée,
Il a guetté les jolies filles après danser
Mais tu connais il avait grand envie
Mais pauvre petit Johnny peut pas danser.

Young performers are making their presence known on the Cajun music
scene, gradually replacing older musicians on the weekend dance hall circuit
and representing traditional Cajun music at local and national festivals.
Some, like Bruce Daigrepont, Wayne Toups and his ZydeCajun band, and
Filé are innovating daring new sounds and styles from recombinations of old
and new elements. Some of the words of these new songs question the
wholesale buying of the American Dream:

Et c'est pas de l'argent qui va te faire content.
Quand j'avais de l'argent, j'ai passé des mauvais temps.
Et c'est pas des piastres qui va te faire heureux.
Quand j'étais millionaire, j'étais un pauvre malheureux.

Quand j'étais millionaire, j'avais les femmes que je voulais.
J'avais des jolies blondes, des p'tites brunes et des têtes rouges.
J'avais quelque chose que je manquais
Jusqu'à j'ai trouvé la belle p'tite veuve sur la Rivière Rouge.

Et c'est pas de l'argent qui va te faire content.
Quand j'avais de l'argent, j'ai passé des mauvais temps.
Et c'est pas des piastres qui va te faire heureux.
Quand j'étais millionaire, j'étais un pauvre malheureux.

Et un soir après gambler, j'ai perdu tout mon argent.
Et j'ai été pour sauter dans la Rivière Rouge.
Une p'tite femme est venue me sauver et le même soir on était marié.
Aujourd'hui la vie est belle sur la Rivière Rouge...

(©Bruce Daigrepont, from "La Valse de la Rivière Rouge," on *Stir Up the*

Roux, Rounder 6016; Bayou Pon Pon Publishing, all rights reserved, used
by permission.)

Bruce Daigrepont shows much social consciousness in his original
compositions. In "Two step de Marksville," he describes the founding of his
family's hometown, while in "Disco and Fais do-do," he reflects specifically
on the loss of cultural and ethnic roots among young Cajuns and Creoles
who missed their water when the well began to run dry:

A peu près cinq ans passés, je pouvais pas espérer
Pour quitter la belle Louisiane.
Quitter ma famille, quitter mon village,
Sortir de la belle Louisiane.
J'aimais pas l'accordéon, j'aimais pas le violon,
Je voulais pas parler le français.
À cette heure, je suis ici dans la Californie.
J"ai changé mon idée.

Je dis, "Hé yaie yaie. Je manque la langue Cadjin.
C'est juste en anglais parmi les Américains.
J'ai manqué Mardi Gras. Je mange pas du gombo.
Et je vas au disco, mais je manque le fais do-do.

J'avais l'habitude de changer la station
Quand j'entendais les chansons cadjins.
Moi, je voulais entendre la même musique,
Pareil comme les Américains.
À cette heure, je m'ennuie de les vieux Cadjins.
C'est souvent je joue leurs disques.

Et moi, je donnerais à peu près deux cents piastres
Pour une livre des écrevisses...

Wayne Toups came up through the ranks, playing dancehalls in prairie towns like Riceville and Rayne. His heroes include such notables as Iry Lejeune, Nathan Abshire and Belton Richard. On this solid foundation, he is building new structures. Besides adding dynamic new arrangements to Cajun standards, he has learned to create within the tradition. "Soigne mes enfants" and "Mon ami" are among the most beautiful Cajun waltzes of this decade.

J'étais assis après jongler une journée
Ça qu'a arrivé avec mon ami longtemps passé.
Il était un musicien proche toute sa vie
Jusqu'à sa femme l'a quitté avec sa petite fille.

Il dit, "Pourquoi tu me fais ça?
Tu connais les larmes vont tomber.
Pourquoi tu reviens pas avec moi à la maison
Une autre fois, petit cœur, pour une autre chance?"

Wayne Toups' recent contract with Polygram Records has brought Cajun music to a new segment of the American public, the MTV crowd. Meanwhile, back home in Louisiana, his highly original style has influenced many young musicians who hear in his music a blend of traditional and up-to-the-minute contemporary sounds.

And the beat goes on. One band called Mamou is experimenting with a combination of Cajun and rock without accordions or fiddles. Others, like Steve Riley, Robert Jardell, Felix and Sterling Richard, express a strong interest in reverently preserving the style and repertoires of their mentors, yet even these constantly recharge past songs with the vitality of the present. Some, like Felton Lejeune, Eddie Lejeune, and Ervin Lejeune, unselfconsciously carry on venerable family and neighborhood traditions. A few, such as Joel Sonnier and Bessyl Duhon, have left home for larger markets, but maintain close contact with their roots. Still others, like Jambalaya and Paul Daigle and Cajun Gold, stay home and keep feverishly busy producing new songs for the local music scene where the true value of a song is demonstrated by how many other bands use it in their weekly dance hall performances. Jambalaya combines the creative talents of Terry and Tony Huval, Reggie Matte, Ken David and Bobby Dumatrait on popular new songs such as "La Mazurka" and "La Belle de la campagne," while Paul Daigle's group has made excellent use of Pierre Varmon Daigle's recent wellspring of new songs, many of which have already become dance band standards, including "La Valse de la vie," "La Nouvelle Valse d'anniversaire," and "La Lumière dans ton chassis."

J'ai été pour voir la lumière dans ton chassis.
Quand je la voyais, c'était un signe que toi, t'étais seule.
Ton mari était pas là et toi, tu m'espérais.
J'allais te joindre, 'tite fille, avec un cœur aussi content.

J'étais sûr t'étais la seule que mon cœur pouvait aimer.
J'étais sûr moi, j'étais le seul que toi, tu voulais.
J'ai quitté ma femme et toi, ton mari.
On s'a marié ensemble, 'tite fille, et mon cœur était content.

Mon vieux père, il m'avait dit, "Fais attention, mon garçon.
La lumière pour toi à soir peut être pour l'autre avant longtemps.
Il y a des femmes qu'est comme ça. Ça aime montrer leur lumière.
La lumière pour toi à soir peut être pour l'autre demain au soir.

Hier soir, j'étais caché pour guetter ta lumière.
Elle a resté allumée jusqu'à j'ai vu lui arriver.
Je suis toujours après guetter la lumière dans ton chassis,
Mais à soir je la guette avec un cœur aussi cassé.

In the late 1980s, the experimentation process has accelerated. Even a self-avowed traditionalist like Michael Doucet has origins in rock and roll. In the early 1970s, his short-lived group Coteau was one of the first groups to tamper with instrumentation and arrangements, adding hard-driving rock influences to traditional songs. His steady group Beausoleil has long folded jazz and rock into their sound. Doucet has also teamed up with a new group called Cajun Brew, with Pat Breaux on accordion and sax, Jimmy Breaux on drums, Sonny Landreth on electric slide and Steve LaCroix on bass, to record Cajun French versions of 1960s rock songs, such as "Louie Louie" and "Wooly Bully." Mamou, named for the hometown of bandleader Steve Lafleur, has taken the Cajun sound to its current extreme. The style of his electric guitar leads is clearly influenced by rock greats such as Jimi Hendrix and Eric Clapton, yet his rendition of Cajun classics such as "La Valse des Balfa" and "La Danse de Mardi Gras" on his recent album (*Mamou,* Jungle Records 1010) are familiar, not only in melody, but in spirit as well.

Even some of the most conservative elements in Cajun music, like Dewey Balfa himself, insist that tradition is not a product but a process and continue to produce new songs and styles from within the culture. While performing at the 1985 Smithsonian Festival of American Folklife, Dewey surprised the audience by announcing that he was going to play a few original songs from his *Souvenirs* album. He went on to explain:

> Cajun music is like a tree. Its roots have to be watered or it will die. But watering the roots is not all. If a tree is alive, it will grow, and that growth is important, too. Most of the songs I play are about a hundred years old. I'm interested in preserving Cajun music. I've dedicated my life to try to assure that there will be lots of Cajun musicians in another hundred years. But that's not enough. Someone has to provide them with songs to play that will be about a hundred years old then, so I've composed a few that I hope will still be around.

The audience was relieved to hear that these new songs, such as "J'ai pleuré" and "Quand j'étais pauvre," sounded like traditional Cajun music. They sounded that way because they were traditional, coming from the same process which produced the older songs. One of those songs reflects persistent concerns about money and real human values, concerns similar to those expressed by Bruce Daigrepont above, as well as Dewey Balfa's own playful observations about aging and courting:

Et quand j'étais petit,
Joli et bien capable,
A cause que j'étais pauvre,
Personne voulait pas me voir.

Et là j'ai eu la chance,
Je m'ai fait un peu d'argent.
N'importe ayoù je peux aller,
Ça veut tout courtiser.

Quand même je suis pas joli,
Quand même je suis pas capable.
D'abord que j'ai de l'argent.
Ça veut tout courtiser.

(©Dewey Balfa, "Et quand j'étais pauvre," on *Souvenirs*, Swallow 6056;
Flat Town Music; all rights reserved; used by permission.)

Purists who would resist new instrumentation, styles and compositions
neglect to consider that change and innovation have always been an integral
part of Cajun music. Those who want to freeze the tradition at any point
lack an historical perspective and share a basic misunderstanding of the
importance of improvisation and the creolization process in French
Louisiana in general and in Cajun music in particular. The same approach
would have barred the borrowing of Anglo-American ballads and Spanish
tunes in the eighteenth century, the introduction of the accordion in the
nineteenth century, the adding of other instruments in the 1940s and 1950s,
the influence of the blues, the addition of swing and country sounds along
the way. Today the blending and fusion at the heart of the development of
Cajun culture continue to be essential to its music. As Wayne Toups
described his own creative input within the traditional context: "There is
room to maneuver, but there are clear borders. You can go a long way as
long as you respect those borders."

Selected Bibliography

Ancelet, Barry Jean, and Elemore Morgan, Jr. *The Makers of Cajun Music.*
Austin: University of Texas Press, 1984.
Brasseaux, Carl A. *The Founding of New Acadia: Beginnings of Acadian Life
in Louisiana, 1765-1803.* Baton Rouge: Louisiana State University Press,
1987.
Broven, John. *South to Louisiana: The Music of the Cajun Bayous.* Gretna,
La.: Pelican Publishing Company, 1983.
Conrad, Glenn R., ed. *The Cajuns: Essays on the History and Culture.*
Lafayette: University of Southwestern Louisiana, Center for Louisiana
Studies Publications, 1978; third edition, 1983.
Dormon, James H. *The People Called Cajuns.* Lafayette: University of
Southwestern Louisiana, Center for Louisiana Studies Publications, 1983.
Guillot, Johnny Allan. *Memories.*
Savoy, Ann Allen. *Cajun Music: A Reflection of A People.* Eunice, La.:
Bluebird Publishing, 1985.
Whitfield, Irene Thérèse. *Louisiana French Folk Songs.* Baton Rouge:
Louisiana State University Press, 1939; third edition, Church Point, La.,
1981.

Reference Discography

The following discography is not intended to be encyclopedic. Entries refer
to recordings of songs and/or musicians mentioned in the text for readers
interested in hearing the music discussed in this presentation. Only albums
(33 rpm) that are readily available are included; historic 78s and 45s are not
listed. Complete catalogs may be obtained from individual record companies.
Among the most complete mail order sources for recordings of Cajun music
and zydeco are:

Floyd's Record Shop
P. O. Drawer 10
Ville Platte, LA 70586

Down Home Music
10341 San Pablo Avenue
El Cerrito, CA 94530

Roundup Records
P. O. Box 154 Dept I
North Cambridge, MA 02140

CAJUN MUSIC

Anthologies

Festival de Musique Acadienne, '81: Live (Swallow 6046)

Folksongs of the Louisiana Acadians, vols. 1 and 2 (Arhoolie 5009 and 5015)

J'étais au bal (Swallow 6020)

Louisiana Cajun French Music Association: Laisse le bon temps rouler, vol. 1 (CFMA Records 02)

Louisiana Cajun Music, vol. 1: The First Recordings (Old Timey 108)

Louisiana Cajun Music, vol. 2: The Early '30s (Old Timey 109)

Louisiana Cajun Music, vol. 3: The String Bands of the 1930s (Old Timey 110)

Louisiana Cajun Music, vol. 4: From the '30s to the '50s (Old Timey 111)

Louisiana Cajun Music, vol. 5: The Early Years, 1928-1932 (Old Timey 114)

Louisiana Cajun and Creole Music, 1934: The Lomax Recordings (Swallow 8003-2)

Nathan Abshire

Pine Grove Blues (Swallow 6014)

The Good Times Are Killing Me (Swallow 6023)

A Cajun Legend: The Best of Nathan Abshire (Swallow 6061)

A Cajun Tradition, vol. 1 (La Louisianne 139)
                                        vol. 2 (La Louisianne 144)

Nathan Abshire (Arhoolie 5013)

Alphonse "Bois-sec" Ardoin and the Ardoin Family Band

La Musique créole (Arhoolie 1070)

Amédé Ardoin

Original 1928-38 Recordings (Old Timey 124)

Vin Bruce

Jole Blon (Swallow 6002)

Greatest Hits (Swallow 6006)

Cajun Country (Swallow 6015)

Dewey Balfa and the Balfa Brothers

Traditional Cajun Music (Swallow 6011)

More Traditional Cajun Music (Swallow 6019)

The New York Concerts (Swallow 6037)

Souvenirs (Swallow 6056)

The Balfa Brothers (Rounder 6007)

Under the Green Oak Tree (Arhoolie 5019), with Marc Savoy and D. L. Menard

Joe Bonsall and the Orange Playboys

Joe Bonsall's Greatest Hits (Swallow 6049)

Harry Choates

   Harry Choates: Original 1946-49 Recordings (Arhoolie 5027)
   Jole Blon (D 7000)

Paul Daigle and Cajun Gold

   The Cajun Experience (Swallow 6058), with Michael Doucet
   Cajun Gold (Swallow 6060)
   The Light in Your Window (Swallow 6068)
   Cœur Farouche (Swallow 6077)

Bruce Daigrepont

   Stir Up the Roux (Rounder 6016)

Michael Doucet and Beausoleil

   The Spirit of Cajun Music (Swallow 6031)
   Zydeco Gris Gris (Swallow 6054)
   Dit Beausoleil (Arhoolie 5025)
   Michael Doucet with Beausoleil (Arhoolie 5034)
   Allons à Lafayette (Arhoolie 5036)
   Hot Chili Mama (Arhoolie 5040)
   Bayou Boogie (Rounder 6015)
   Michael Doucet and Cajun Brew (Rounder 6017)

Joseph and Cléoma Falcon

   Louisiana Cajun Music (Arhoolie 5005)
   Cléoma B. Falcon: A Cajun Music Classic (Jadfel 101)

Filé

   Cajun Dance Band (Flying Fish 418)

Canray Fontenot

   Fiddle Styles, vol. 1 (Arhoolie 5031)

Chuck Guillory

   Grand Texas (Arhoolie 5039)

Hackberry Ramblers

   Louisiana Cajun Music (Arhoolie 5003)

Jambalaya

   Le Nouvel Esprit de la Musique Cadien (Swallow 6075)

Doug Kershaw

>*The Louisiana Man* (Warner Brothers 3166)
>*Alive and Pickin'* (Warner Brothers 2851)
>*The Cajun Way* (Warner Brothers 1820)

Adam and Cyprien Landreneau

>*Cajun Sole* (Swallow 8001)

Eddie LeJeune

>*Cajun Soul* (Rounder 6013)

Iry LeJeune

>*The Legendary Iry LeJeune*, vol. 1 (Goldband 7740)
>*The Legendary Iry LeJeune*, vol. 2 (Goldband 7741)

Mamou

>*Mamou* (Jungle Records 1010)

Dennis McGee and Sady Courville

>*Dennis McGee: The Early Recordings* (Morning Star 45002)
>*La Vieille Musique Acadienne* (Swallow 6030)

D. L. Menard

>*The Louisiana Aces* (Arhoolie 6003)
>*The Back Door* (Swallow 6038)
>*No Matter Where You At* (Rounder 6021)

Michot Brothers

>*Élevés à Pilette* (RZ 1014)

Jimmy C. Newman

>*Cajun and Country, Too* (Swallow 6052)
>*Lache pas la patate* (La Louisianne 140)

Austin Pitre

>*The Evangeline Playboys* (Swallow 6041)

Belton Richard

>*Belton Richard and the Musical Aces* (Swallow 6010)
>*Belton Richard*, vol. 2 (Swallow 6013)

Good 'n Cajun (Swallow 6021)
Louisiana Cajun Music (Swallow 6032)
At His Best (Swallow 6043)

Felix and Sterling Richard, the Cankton Express

Traditional Cajun Music (Swallow 6073)

Zachary Richard

Bayou des Mystères (Kébec Disc KD 913)
Mardi Gras (RZ 1005)
Allons Danser (RZ 1007)
Live in Montréal (RZ 1003)
Vent d'Été (Kébec Disc KD 541)
Zack Attack (RZ 1009)
Looking Back (RZ 1011)

Gene Rodrigue

The Bayou Cajun Music (Swallow 6062)

Aldus Roger and the Lafayette Playboys

Aldus Roger Plays French Music (La Louisianne 107)
King of the French Accordion (La Louisianne 114)
Aldus Roger Plays Cajun French Classics (La Louisianne 122)

Marc Savoy

Oh What a Night! (Arhoolie 5023)
Savoy Doucet Cajun Band (Arhoolie 5029), with Michael Doucet
Savoy Doucet with Spirits (Arhoolie 5037), with Michael Doucet

Leo Soileau

Original 1930s Recordings (Old Timey 125)

Joel Sonnier

Cajun Life (Rounder 3049)

Rufus Thibodeaux

The Cajun Country Fiddle (La Louisianne 129)
Cajun Fiddle (La Louisianne 137)

Wayne Toups and ZydeCajun

Wayne Toups ZydeCajun (MTE 5032)
Johnnie Can't Dance (MTE 5035)

Blast from the Bayou (Polygram 8365181)

Lawrence Walker

A Legend At Last (Swallow 6051)
Tribute to the Late, Great Lawrence Walker (La Louisianne 126)

SWAMP POP

Anthologies

Rockin' Date with South Louisiana Stars (Jinn 4002)
South Louisiana Juke Box Hits (Jinn 4006)
More South Louisiana Juke Box Favorites (Jinn 4010)
Golden Dozen Hits (Jinn 9001)
Golden Dozen, vol. 2 (Jinn 9004)
                              vol. 3 (Jinn 9013)
                              vol. 4 (Jinn 9020)
Cajun and Swamp Pop Super Hits (Jinn 9028)

Johnnie Allan

South to Louisiana (Jinn 4001)
Johnnie Allan Sings (Jinn 9002)
Dedicated to You (Jinn 9006)
A Portrait of Johnnie Allan (Jinn 9012)
Another Man's Woman (Jinn 9015)
Johnnie Allan's Greatest Hits (Jinn 9017)
Louisiana Swamp Fox (Jinn 9019)
Cajun Country (Jinn 9022)
Thanks for the Memories (Jinn 9026)

Rod Bernard

Rod Bernard (Jinn 4007)
Country Lovin' (Jinn 9008)
Boogie in Black and White (Jinn 9014), with Clifton Chenier

Boogie Kings

The Boogie Kings (MN 104)
Blue Eyed Soul (MN 109)
Boogie Kings Live at the Bamboo Hut (MN 111)

Cookie and the Cupcakes

3 Great Rockers (Jinn 9003), with Shelton Dunaway and Lil Alfred
Cookie and the Cupcakes, vol. 2 (Jinn 9018)

Dale and Grace

   I'm Leaving It Up to You (MN 100)

Clint West

   Clint West and the Boogie Kings (Jinn 4003)
   The Fabulous Kings (Jinn 4004)
   Clint West (Jinn 9005)